Double Knitting

Reversible Two-Color Designs

by

M'Lou Baber

DOUBLE KNITTING

REVERSIBLE TWO-COLOR DESIGNS

BY

M'LOU BABER

models: Cecilia Monroy, Renata Monroy, Katherine Olson, Lloie Schwartz, Elizabeth Spellman, Michelle Wolfe

photographer: Meg Swansen

pattern-writer: Amy Detjen

technical editors: Amy Detjen, Joyce Williams

proof readers: Tami Schiferl, Joyce Williams

charts realized by Amy Detjen, with *Stitch Painter* from Cochinelle Studio

schematics realized by Michael delVecchio with *Adobe Illustrator*

Cover design, photo editing and pre-press by JLS Photography & Graphic Design

editorial assistant: Michelle Wolfe

The coats on pages 74 and 106 were knitted by Jane Hill in Finnish *Satakieli* wool from Schoolhouse Press.

The Art Deco Coat on page 130, knitted by M'Lou Baber, is from the private collection of Karen Kress.

Photography locations in Marshfield, Wisconsin: Foxfire Botanical Gardens, Thimbleberry Bookstore, The Kitchen Table restaurant and the Marshfield Clinic; our thanks to them all.

The painting on the exterior wall of The Kitchen Table restaurant (pages 38 and 42) is by Gene Wesley. All watercolors by M'Lou Baber.

ISBN-10: 0-942018-28-1
ISBN-13: 978-0-942018-28-8

Library of Congress Control Number: 2008928938

printed in the U.S.A. by Worzalla

Schoolhouse Press
6899 Cary Bluff
Pittsville, WI 54466
(715) 884-2799
www.schoolhousepress.com

ECO-FRIENDLY BOOKS
Made in the USA

Table of Contents

Introduction

In October 1984 I picked up the holiday issue of *McCall's Needlework and Crafts* magazine and found a red and white afghan with Santa in his sleigh among the snowflakes. How could I resist? But it was knitted in a way I had never seen: a double stitch that made the afghan reversible. I bought the magazine and tried a swatch. The technique worked; it was fun; it was fast; I was hooked.

After that first Christmas blanket, I realized I could design my own and knitted a slew of blankets for my grandchildren.

I then searched for books or instructions on how to double-knit garments and even wrote to McCall's, but could find nothing. Could I design my own?

Because of what I had learned while Double Knitting so many blankets, I knew the garments would need to be outerwear; the air pocket between the two sides creates automatic insulation. The worsted weight wool I had used for the blankets had, in the past, always worked up at 5 stitches to the inch in plain stockinette stitch -- but Double Knitting had produced 3-1/2 stitches to the inch. So, if I wanted 5 stitches to the inch, I would have to choose a considerably lighter-weight yarn.

I began to experiment with children's sweaters, roughly following the recommended sizes, but charting new designs to my heart's content. Graphing is one of my favorite occupations; doodles which are doubled or tripled or mirror-imaged or overlapped become new motifs. I have designed new charts with pencil and squared paper until my back hurt; I had writer's cramp and couldn't sleep for the squares flowing through my mind. Now, with computer-generated charting programs, it is considerably easier to experiment.

Finding the right yarn is important. Double Knitting can be heavy and requires a loosely-plied, light-weight yarn. DK or sport weight mohair blend yarns work very well; worsted weight is almost too dense for clothing.

Double Knitting produces a wide stitch which makes swatching especially important. If you want to convert an existing, single-yarn design to Double Knitting, the gauge will be very different. I will often go down two needle sizes to get the gauge I want; if I tighten up too much, the fabric becomes heavy. It is a very delicate balance and requires swatching to discover the right gauge.

To increase and decrease within Double Knitting, you must shape each side of the fabric separately. See *Techniques* on page 12 for more complete details.

What I like best about this technique is working large, intricate motifs without stranding the yarns. A blank piece of graph paper thrills me as much as blank watercolor paper.

The joys of knitting are endless; casting off rules gives us the freedom to be creative. Go for it!

Getting Gauge

Double Knitting produces a *much* wider gauge than a single-layer stockinette stitch fabric. This means you may have to go down several needle sizes to get the gauge that is recommended for a specific yarn. It is essential that you knit a sample swatch, even if you are not typically a knitter who swatches.

For example, if the yarn label recommends a gauge of 24 stitches and 38 rows to 4", you may get 20 DSPs (Double-Stitch Pairs) and 26 rows to 4".

Go Figure;
Estimating the Amount of Yarn Needed

There I was, just about halfway through a lap robe and I realized I was going to run out of yarn. Of course I had found the yarn on sale; there was no more at the store. I finished the blanket and it was fine, but I had wanted it to be twice as big. I needed to figure out how to determine yardage before beginning a project.

For a month I made 4" squares of Double Knitting with all my scraps and various needles. Then, I cut off the end and ripped each square apart and measured the number of yards in each square. I know just enough about math to know that there must be formula in there somewhere.

My brilliant nephew, Evan, is a math whiz and I knew he could figure it out for me. I supposed that, if we knew how many yards it took to make a 4" square and if we knew how many stitches were in an entire coat, we could determine the yardage necessary to make a coat.

It worked. Evan and I didn't really talk the same language, but I was able to translate his math into my Knitter's Math and here is the result.

To estimate yardage required for an entire garment:

1. Determine the number of stitches in the project (P) you are knitting: see the formula below.

> For this example, we'll use a coat with the following numbers:
> The chart has 210 sts and 176 rows (210 x 176) = 36,960 sts
> The sleeve chart has 100 sts x 85 rows x 2 sleeves (100 x 85 x 2) = 17,000 sts
> The cuff is 50 sts x 10 rows x 2 sleeves (50 x 10 x 2) = 1,000 sts
> Add them up, and the total sts in the project is 54,960; this is **P**.

2. Using 1 skein of each color, knit a sample until you find the gauge you want for that yarn.
3. Using that gauge, cast on a swatch that will be 4" wide.
4. DK until the swatch is 4" tall.
5. Note the number of stitches (S) and rows (R) in your swatch and multiply them to get **X**.
6. Rip your swatch (ouch), and measure one of the two colors of yarn. This is **Y**. Make sure you note this in number of yards, not number of feet.
7. Divide **X** by **Y**, so you know how many stitches you get from only one yard; this is **Z**.

$$\frac{S \times R = X}{Y} = Z$$

S = number of sts (width) of your 4" swatch
R = number of rows (height) of your 4" swatch
X = total number of sts in your 4" square swatch (**S x R**)
Y = number of yards (1 color only) needed to knit your 4" square swatch
Z = number of sts you get from 1 yard of yarn

8. Divide the number of stitches in the project (**P**) by the number of stitches you get in one yard (**Z**). You now have the yardage needed for each color to knit the entire piece.

$$P \div Z = \text{yards needed for each color}$$

> A graphic example:
>
> My 4" square swatch is 20 sts wide and 24 rows tall. When I ripped it out, each color had used 12 yards of yarn.
> To calculate **Z**:
>
> $$\frac{20 \times 24 = 480}{12} = 40 \text{ (Z)}$$
>
> **S** = 20 (number of sts in my swatch)
> **R** = 24 (number of rows in my swatch)
> **X** = 480 (total number of stitches in my swatch (**S x R**))
> **Y** = number of yards (1 color only) I used to knit my swatch
> **Z** = number of sts I got from 1 yard of each color

This is just an estimate, and you should always buy more than you think you'll need, just in case.
The whole process makes me feel powerful.

Abbreviations & Definitions

approx	approximately
back	Double Knitting is completely reversible, so there is technically no "front" or "back". In this text, "back" refers to the side of the fabric that is farthest from you while working that row.
BO sep	Bind Off separately - use color A to bind off knit stitches, use color B to bind off purl stitches. See *Binding Off* on page 13.
BO tog	Bind Off together - use colors A and B together to bind off a Pair (as if it were one stitch). See *Binding Off* on page 13.
byb	both yarns back - Put both yarns to the far side of your work, but knit with only one.
byf	both yarns forward - Bring both yarns to the front of your work, but purl with only one.
CES	Closed Edge Stitch - Use this option to keep side A and side B joined at the edge of the fabric. See *Edge Stitches* on page 14.
CO	Cast on
colors A & B	Color A refers to the white boxes on the chart, color B refers to the black boxes on the charts. See *Reading Charts* on page 17.
cont	continue
cork	Put a stopper (such as a cork) onto the needle to keep stitches from escaping.
dec	decrease - See **Decreasing DSPs** on page 13
dec 1 DSP	Decrease 1 Double-Stitch Pair (see *Decreasing DSPs* on page 13)
DK	Double Knit (verb) - Perform a knit stitch with one color and a purl stitch with the other; DK *x* means Double Knit *x* pairs. See *Working DSPs* on page 11 for more information.
dp(n)	double-pointed (needle)
DSP	Double-Stitch Pair (noun) - This is a pair of stitches on your needle: a knit stitch in one color and a purl stitch in the other. This pair is treated as one unit.
ES	Edge Stitch
front	Double Knitting is completely reversible, so there is technically no "front" or "back". In this text, "front" refers to the side of the fabric that is facing you while working that row.
inc	increase - See *Increasing DSPs* on page 11.
k	knit
knit up	Use a new strand of yarn to knit up stitches along an edge (see *Pick Up vs Knit Up* on page 16).
k'wise	knitwise, or "as if to knit"
OES	Open Edge Stitch - Use this option to keep side A and side B separate at the edge of the fabric. See *Edge Stitches* on page 14.
pair	This is a short form of DSP.
pick up	Pick up stitches along an edge (see *Pick Up vs Knit Up* on page 16).
pivot stitch	This is a stitch that represents a turn in the direction of your knitting. See *Reading Charts* on page 17 for more information.
pm	place marker
p'wise	purlwise, or "as if to purl"
sep	separate
sides A & B	Side A refers to the pattern as shown on the chart. Side B is the negative image of Side A (see *Reading Charts* on page 17).
sl	Slip a stitch p'wise (as if to purl) unless otherwise indicated.
tog	together, as in knit 2 together (k2tog), or purl 2 together (p2tog)
tie on	When starting the second color, loosely tie it to the first color and begin to knit.
work	Continue to knit or Double Knit the stitches as established: "work 8 DSPs" is synonymous with "DK 8 pairs".

DOUBLE KNITTING

Techniques

Double Knitting creates a reversible, two-layer fabric; both sides show only knit stitches. The purl sides of the two layers face the inside, and there are air pockets between them. The finished fabric is lofty and warm, making it perfect for outerwear, yet it is seldom heavy.

When you work a two-color design in Double Knitting, the two layers are intertwined at each color change. Because you use both colors to work each pair of stitches, there are no strands across the back of the fabric. All leftover yarn ends are tucked into the air pockets so the finished article is neat and tidy on both sides.

As with other types of knitting where you use two strands, you can hold both yarns in one hand, or one in each hand. These photos show Double Knitting holding one color in each hand.

At present, there are some innovative knitters experimenting with working a different motif on each surface; we watch with interest.

The garments in this book are totally reversible; in both design and construction. This effect takes special attention to edge stitches and shoulder seams, but all is revealed in the following pages.

Some of the charts are rather small; you have our permission to enlarge them for your personal use only.

Casting On for Double Knitting

Each DSP (Double-Stitch Pair) consists of a knit stitch in one color and a purl stitch in the opposite color. This pair is considered one unit. If you want to begin Double Knitting immediately after casting on, the following method is the easiest:

Cast On with 2 Strands - Using 2 strands of one color held together, CO 1 stitch for each DSP you need. You now have pairs of stitches ready to begin Double Knitting (see Photo 1).

Photo 1

Treat each strand of yarn as one stitch (half of a pair). If you prefer, you may use the cast-on of your choice and then use one of the methods described in Establishing DSPs (as follows).

Establishing DSPs
(Double-Stitch Pairs)

If you start with a single-layer border of ribbing or a pattern stitch, you need to double the number of stitches on your needle to begin Double Knitting. You can also use either of these methods above any cast-on edge.

Method 1: Use One Color to Double the Number of Stitches
With one color, work one row (or round) as follows: *k and p into next stitch, repeat from *. This doubles the number of stitches you have on your needle and establishes DSPs.

Method 2: Use Both Colors to Double the Number of Stitches
This method is similar to Method 1, but uses both colors to establish the DSPs; it is best used above the last row of a border such as Ribbing or Seed Stitch.

Loosely tie on second color. *Byb (both yarns back), knit the first stitch and leave it on the left-hand needle. Byf (both yarns forward), using other color, purl the same stitch and remove it from the left-hand needle. Repeat from * to the end of row. This turns each stitch of the foundation row into a DSP.

Working DSPs (Double-Stitch Pairs) a.k.a. Double Knitting

When working DSPs, always knit on the side closest to you, and purl on the side that is away from you. When you're following a color chart, every square represents one DSP. Each pair consists of a knit of one color and a purl of the opposite color.

1. Byb (both yarns back), knit the knit stitch using the appropriate color (see Photo 2).

Photo 2

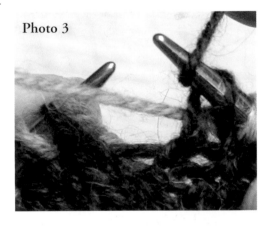

2. Byf, (see Photo 3), purl the purl stitch using the opposite color (see Photo 4).

Photo 3

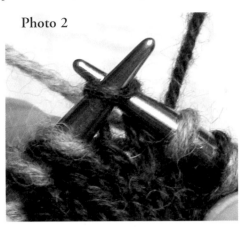

Photo 4

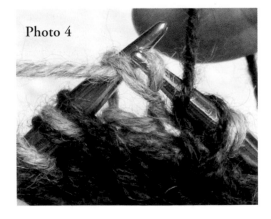

Increasing DSPs

Just as in single-layer knitting, there are several ways to increase stitches in Double Knitting. Unless the instructions specify a particular type of increase, use whichever method is easiest for you.

Method 1: Increase from the Row Below

This is my favorite increase.

1. Prior to a knit stitch, byf (both yarns forward), from behind, identify the stitch below the next purl stitch on left-hand needle (see Photo 5).

Photo 5

2. With tip of right-hand, lift the right side of that stitch onto left-hand needle (see Photo 6).

Photo 6

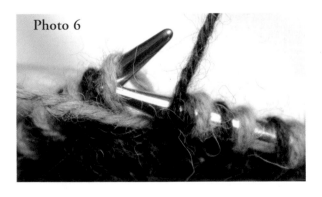

3. Byb (both yarns back), on front of work identify stitch below next knit stitch on left-hand needle (see Photo 7). With tip of right-hand needle, lift right side of that stitch onto left-hand needle. You have added one stitch to side A and one stitch to side B.

Photo 7

4. Continue DK. Photo 8 shows the two lifted stitches on left-hand needle, ready to work.

Photo 8

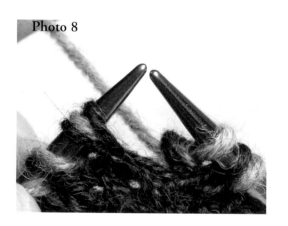

Method 2: Make One Increase

This is the same as the M1 increase used in single-layer knitting, but you perform it once for the front layer and once for the back layer.

1. Byb, use the tip of the right-hand needle to lift the horizontal bar between the last knit stitch you worked and the next knit stitch (see Photo 9). Knit into the back of that loop with appropriate color.

Photo 9

2. Byf, use the tip of the left-hand needle to lift the horizontal bar between the last purl stitch you worked and the next purl stitch (see Photo 10). Purl into the back of that loop with appropriate color.

Photo 10

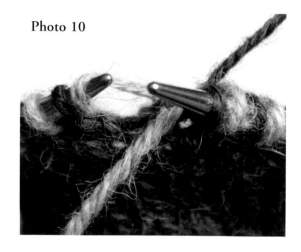

DOUBLE KNITTING

Decreasing DSPs

Decrease DSPs by knitting two knit stitches together, and purling two purl stitches together. Before you can do this, you must rearrange the stitches so that the 2 knits are side-by-side and the 2 purls are side-by-side:

1. Slip the next knit stitch from the left-hand needle to the right-hand needle.

2. Slip the next purl stitch onto a cable needle and hold it in back (see Photo 11).

Photo 11

3. Return the knit stitch to the left-hand needle.

4. Byb, using appropriate color, k2tog.

5. Place the purl stitch from the cable needle back onto the left-hand needle (see Photo 12).

6. Byf, p2tog using appropriate color.

You have decreased 1 DSP.

Photo 12

Note: If you prefer another decrease method, such as ssk, use that. Remember to perform it once on the side closest to you, and once on the other side.

Binding Off

There are two different ways to bind off in Double Knitting:

Method 1: Bind Off Together (BO tog)

This is the method you use to unite the front and back layers as you bind off. After the last row, drop one color. Using the other color only, *k1, p1, repeat from * to end of row. Turn. K2tog (you are knitting a knit stitch together with a purl stitch), *k2tog, pass first stitch on right needle over second, repeat from * across row.

Method 2: Bind Off Separately (BO sep)

Use this method for shoulders (or see *Weaving Shoulders* on page 14 for an alternate method).

Use 2 dp or circular needles and separate the knit stitches and the purl stitches (see Photo 13). Using appropriate color, bind off the knit stitches. Using other color, bind off the purl stitches in purl.

Photo 13

Weaving Shoulders (Alternative to BO Sep)

Instead of binding off for shoulders, as written in most of the patterns in this book, you may opt to leave the shoulder stitches live and weave (Kitchener stitch) them together to make a more seamless garment.

To do that, do not bind off shoulder stitches as directed, but move them to a holder instead. When the directions tell you to "BO sep 8 DSPs, continue DK to end of row", work the 8 DSPs, then move them to a holder instead of binding off. Continue with the directions, adding more stitches to the holder on subsequent rows.

After you work both the front and back shoulders, prepare to weave them as follows: separate the knit and purl stitches as shown in Photo 13. Weave the stitches from side A front to side A back, being careful not to catch side B. Turn the garment to the other side and weave together side B front and side B back.

This keeps the fabric both reversible and seamless.

Edge Stitches

There are two different edge stitches used in this book:

Closed Edge Stitch (CES)

This is what I use at the front edge of a jacket or coat. At the beginning of each row, with both yarns in the back of your work (byb), slip one stitch (not pair) p'wise. Twist the two yarns so there isn't any hole, and work the row in Double Knitting until a single stitch remains.

At the end of each row, drop color B on the side of your work closest to you and, using color A only, knit the last single stitch (not pair). Photo 14 shows the edge of the color B side (where the edge stitch was worked with color A).

Photo 14

See also *Reading Charts* on page 17 for notes about how edge stitches appear on charts.

Open Edge Stitch (OES)

This is the edge I use when I'm going to be picking up stitches in Double Knitting for a collar or to knit sleeves from the top down. Double Knit to the last pair as shown on the chart. When you turn to work back, make sure that you don't twist the 2 colors (as you do for a Closed Edge Stitch) so that the two layers of fabric remain separate. See Photo 15.

Photo 15

DOUBLE KNITTING

Two-Color Double-Knit Ribbing

This is used for borders, and is a double-layer fabric. When working Double Knit Ribbing, you have 2 Color A stitches next to each other and 2 color B stitches next to each other for most of the row. This is the opposite of regular Double Knitting, but is correct.

In this ribbing, you perform half of the stitches with one color in front and one color in back as follows:

Row 1: Closed Edge Stitch, *byb, k1 A, byf, p1B. Keep B in front and put A to back, p1 B, k1 A. Repeat from * ending with Closed Edge Stitch.

Row 2: Closed Edge Stitch, *put A in front and B in back, p1 A, k1 B. Byb, k1 B, byf, p1 A. Repeat from * ending with Closed Edge Stitch. Photos 16 and 17 show Two-Color DK Ribbing on both sides.

Tip: After you establish the ribbing, go across the row working a "regular pair, split pair, regular pair, split pair" and so on.
Regular Pair: Byb, k1 with appropriate color, byf, p1 with other color.
Split Pair: Purl color in front and knit color in back, p1, k1.

EZ's Applied I-Cord

When using Elizabeth Zimmermann's method of applying I-Cord after the garment is finished, you may use a matching, or a contrasting color for the cord.

Decide if you want 2-, 3-, or 4-stitch cord. With a smaller-size needle, pick up stitches from the selvage of the finished item. Onto a garment-sized needle, cast on 2 (3, 4) stitches. Immediately transfer them to the left-hand needle (pick-up needle).

* k1 (2, or 3), k2tog through back loops. Replace the 2 (3, or 4) stitches to L needle and repeat from *.

3-stitch I-Cord is illustrated: Photo 18 shows knitting the first cord stitch with the working wool coming from the 3rd stitch; Photo 19 shows k2tog through back loops, being the last cord stitch together with a picked up stitch.

Photo 18

Photo 16

Photo 17

Photo 19

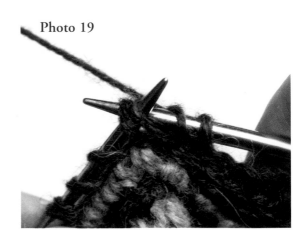

DOUBLE KNITTING

Garter Stitch

This is used for borders, and is a single-layer fabric. To keep the edges even and taut, always knit the last stitch of the row and slip the first stitch p'wise.

Every Row: Sl 1 p'wise, k across row. Turn.

Repeat this row for Garter Stitch.

Moss Stitch

This is used for borders, and is a single-layer fabric. To keep the edges even and taut, always knit the last stitch of the row and slip the first stitch p'wise. These instructions are for working on an even number of stitches.

Row l: Sl 1 p'wise, *k1, p1. Repeat from * ending with k1. Turn.
Row 2: Repeat row 1.
Row 3: Sl 1 p'wise, *p1, k1. Repeat from * until 1 stitch remains, k1. Turn.
Row 4: Repeat row 3.

Repeat Rows 1-4 for Moss Stitch.

Seed Stitch

This is used for borders, and is a single-layer fabric. To keep the edges even and taut, always knit the last stitch of the row and slip the first stitch p'wise. These instructions are for working on an even number of stitches.

Row l: Sl 1 p'wise, *k1, p1, repeat from * ending with k1. Turn.
Row 2: Sl 1 p'wise, *p1, k1, repeat from * until 1 stitch remains, k1. Turn.

Repeat Rows 1 and 2 for Seed Stitch.

Pick Up vs Knit Up

Pick Up: use your needle to pick up a row of stitches along the edge of the work; be consistent.

Knit Up: with the working wool, dive into a half-stitch near the edge of the work and pull the wool through for a new stitch.

K1, P1 Ribbing

This is used for borders, and is a single-layer fabric. To keep the edges even and taut, always knit the last stitch of the row and slip the first stitch p'wise.

With an even number of stitches:

Every Row: Sl 1 p'wise, *k1, p1, repeat from * until 1 stitch remains, k1. Turn.

Repeat this row for K1, P1 Ribbing.

With an odd number of stitches:

Row 1: Sl 1 p'wise, *k1, p1, repeat from * until 1 stitch remains, k1. Turn.

Row 2: Sl 1 p'wise, *p1, k1, repeat from * until 1 stitch remains, k1. Turn.

Repeat these 2 rows for K1, P1 Ribbing.

Making Buttonholes

All of the garments in this book that require buttonholes have borders that are worked in single layer fabric, such as Moss Stitch or Seed Stitch. You may use any buttonhole you like.

Double-Knitting - Slip Method

Although I have never used this method, I've been told that it pre-dates the technique described in this book.

When using only one color: instead of carrying two strands simultaneously and completing both sides of the fabric in one pass, one stitch is knitted and the next stitch is slipped p'wise with wool in front. On the return row, the knitted stitch is slipped and the slipped stitch is knitted. In other words, it takes two passes to complete one row across each layer.

Reading Charts

Double Knitting is achieved by working both layers simultaneously on every row.

Each chart in this book shows the color pattern (motif) on one layer of fabric. The two layers - colorwise - are negative images of each other; stitches shown with white on the chart are worked in black on the other side.

Flat Knitting: As you work back and forth, the layer of fabric that faces you on the second row is the layer that was away from you on the previous row. You need to make a mental adjustment as you read the chart on even-numbered rows. You may find it helpful to place a pin or marker on the side A of your work.

Circular Knitting: If you are working in the round, the same layer of fabric always faces you. Therefore, the chart is read from right to left on all rounds; the knit stitches are always worked as charted and the purl stitches are always worked in the second color.

Chart Squares: Each square on the chart represents one Double-Stitch Pair (DSP). For charts in this book, each pair consists of one stitch in color A and one stitch in color B. Because these designs are all negative images, when you knit with color A on the "front" side, you then purl with color B on the "back" side.

Chart Rows: Each row on the chart represents one row of knitting, but two layers of fabric. The chart represents one side of the fabric; the reverse side is the negative image of that same motif.

Odd-Numbered Rows:
On odd-numbered rows, work the chart from right-to-left exactly as shown: for each white square, k1 with color A and p1 with color B. For each black square, k1 with color B and p1 with color A.

Even-Numbered Rows in Flat Knitting:
On even-numbered rows, work the chart from left-to-right, reversing the colors: for each white square, k1 with color B and p1 with color A. For each black square, k1 with color A and p1 with color B.

Although the rows are not numbered, the "X" boxes along the sides of the charts mark every 10th row. A Magnetic Row Finder is a very useful tool.

Working Motifs: Always begin a new motif with a knit, therefore there will be two stitches of the same color next to each other on the needles - the purl stitch of the previous pair and the knit stitch of the color-change pair.

Pivot Stitches on Charts: When a square on the chart is labeled "Pivot Stitch", that is the mid-point of the row.

Begin the row on the right edge of the chart and work until you have Double Knitted the Pivot Stitch pair. Now read the same row of the chart back from left to right, without repeating the Pivot Stitch.

On charts with a Pivot Stitch, start all rows (even and odd) on the right edge of the chart.

Edge Stitches on Charts: a Closed Edge Stitch is represented by a box with a dot in it. This is a single stitch, not a pair. If the instructions say, "cast on 211 DSPs", you work a Closed Edge stitch, 210 pairs, and a Closed Edge stitch. Therefore, the chart will show 212 stitches across.

Square Coasters or Pot Holders
Learning Double Knitting

The following directions and charts can be used for either a coaster or a pot holder. The only difference between them is gauge (weight of yarn and needle size you choose).

Pot holder: US 6 needles (4.0 mm) and two colors of worsted weight cotton.
Coaster: US 2 needles (2.0 mm) and two colors of fingering weight cotton.

Finished Size:	**Coaster:** 3" square (approximate)
	Pot Holder: 5" square (approximate)
Yarn:	**Coaster:** Fingering weight cotton in 2 colors
	Pot Holder: Worsted weight cotton in 2 colors
Needles:	**Coaster:** US 2 (2.0mm)
	Pot Holder: US 6 (4.0mm)
Gauge:	**Coaster:** 28 DSPs and 28 rows = 4"
	Pot Holder: 20 DSPs and 20 rows = 4"

Begin

With color A, cast on 29 stitches. See *Abbreviations and Definitions* on page 9 for an explanation of "Colors A and B".

Rows 1-3: Work in Seed Stitch (see *Seed Stitch* on page 16).

Row 4: In this row, you need to continue the Seed Stitch borders (3 stitches at each side), and establish Double Knitting (see *Establishing DSPs* on page 10) on the center 23 stitches. Do this as follows: Using color A, sl 1 p'wise, work Seed Stitch for 2 stitches, pm (place marker). Loosely tie on color B. *Byb (both yarns back), using color A, knit the next stitch and leave it on the left-hand needle. Byf (both yarns forward), using color B, purl the same stitch and remove it from the left-hand needle. Repeat from * to last 3 stitches, twist A and B yarns and, using color A only, work stitches in Seed Stitch, k1.

This Legend is for all Coasters and Pot Holders

- ☐ color A on one side, color B on the other
- ■ color B on one side, color A on the other
- ⊡ Seed Stitch border
- · edge stitch
- ▨ dec 1 DSP
- ⊞ inc 1 DSP

Note the significant difference between the stitch/row ratio of the chart to the actual knitting.

Row 5: Begin following one of the charts (begin with row 5). See *Reading Charts* on page 17 for details on following a chart in Double Knitting. Keep the first and last 3 stitches in Seed Stitch. Make sure to twist colors A and B at the beginning and end of DK section on every row. Here is Row 5 spelled out: Sl 1, work 2 stitches in Seed Stitch, twist A and B yarns, DK across to the last 3 stitches, twist A and B yarns and, using color A only, work last 3 stitches in Seed Stitch.

Rows 6-31: DK following chart, keeping first and last 3 stitches in Seed Stitch.

Row 32: Break off color B. With color A, sl 1, work Seed Stitch for 2 stitches. K1, p1 across the center section (46 stitches), work 2 stitches in Seed Stitch, k1.

Row 33: In this row, you need to halve the number of stitches in the center section (all but the 3 border stitches on each side). Do this as follows: Slip first stitch and work 2 stitches in Seed Stitch. Remove the marker. *k2tog, p2tog across center section to last 3 stitches. Work last 3 stitches in Seed Stitch.

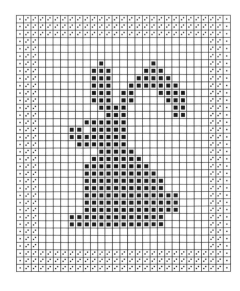
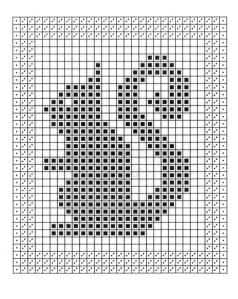

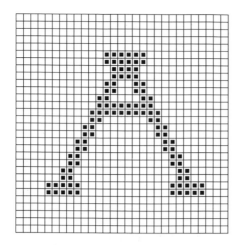

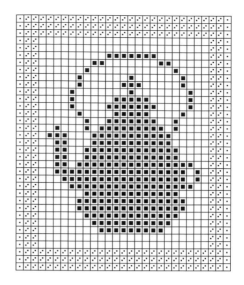

Note: You are decreasing in the Seed Stitch pattern, you may need to start decreasing with p2tog to keep your pattern in tact. Let your knitting dictate whether you start with a k2tog or p2tog.

Rows 34 & 35: Work Seed Stitch.

Finishing: Bind off 29 stitches and tuck any loose ends between front and back fabric.

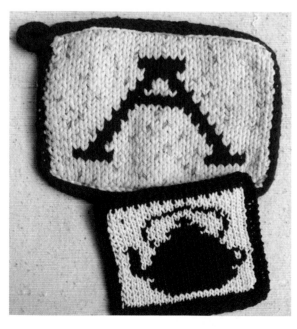

Side A

Side B

DOUBLE KNITTING

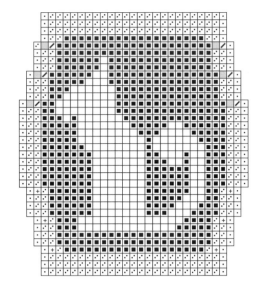
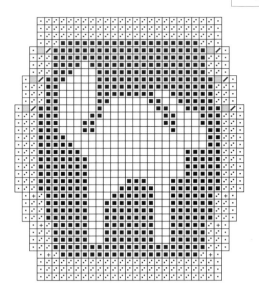

Pot Holder Sample Swatch
Increasing and Decreasing in Double Knitting

Finished Size: 4.5" square (approx)

Yarn: Worsted weight cotton in 2 colors
Needles: US 6 (4.0mm)
Gauge: 20 DSPs and 10 rows = 4"

With color A, cast on 25 stitches. See *Abbreviations and Definitions* on page 9 for an explanation of "Colors A and B".

Rows 1-2: Sl 1, k across row.

Row 3: In this row, you need to continue the Garter Stitch borders (3 stitches at each side), and establish Double Knitting (see *Establishing DSPs* on page 10) on the center 19 stitches. Do this as follows: Using color A, sl 1 knitwise, k2, pm (place marker), k and p into each of the next 19 stitches, pm, k3.

Row 4: Sl 1, k2, loosely tie on color B. DK across row to last 3 stitches, using A, k3.

Row 5, increase row: Sl 1, k2. Increase in next DSP (see *Increasing DSPs* on page 11). DK across to last DSP before marker, increase in next DSP, K3.

Row 6 and on: Follow chart for pattern and color changes. Increase every 4th row twice more (3 increase rows total). DK with no increases for 12 rows. Decrease in the first DSP after the marker and the last DSP before the second marker (see *Decreasing DSPs* on page 13). Continue, following the chart and working decreases as shown.

Next Row: Change back to single-layer knitting as follows: After the last decrease row, break off color B and, using A only, k1, p1 across to second marker. Remove marker and k3.

Next Row: Sl 1, k2tog across to last 3 stitches, k3.

Last 2 Rows: K all stitches. Bind off.

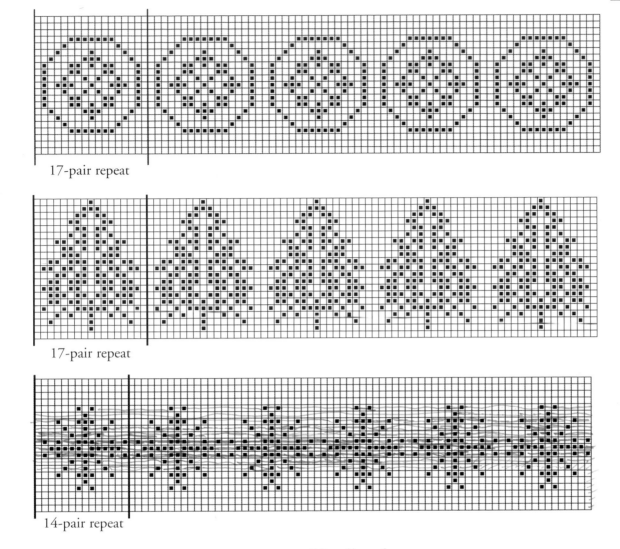

17-pair repeat

17-pair repeat

14-pair repeat

Headband
Knitted in the Round

Finished Size:	20" around (approx)
Yarn:	Sport weight wool or wool blend in 2 colors (one small skein of each color)
Needles:	US 4 (3.5mm)
Gauge:	22 DSPs and 22 rows = 4"

Cast on: With 2 strands of color A held together, cast on 85 sts for Tree or Circles, or 84 sts for Snowflakes. Join into a circle, being careful not to twist the stitches over the needle. Pm for beginning of round. Still using 2 strands of color A held together, work k1, p1 ribbing for 5 rounds.

Round 6: Begin DK as follows: Tie on color B and *byb, k1 with color B, byf, p1 with color A. Repeat from * for entire round, using each strand of the doubled yarn as one stitch. This is the first row of the chart. Follow chart to top.

Next Row: Tie off color B and, with color A only *k1, p1, repeat from * to marker.

Next Row: On the next row K a pair tog, then p a pair tog, creating a rib. Rib with "A" only for 4 more rows and bind off.

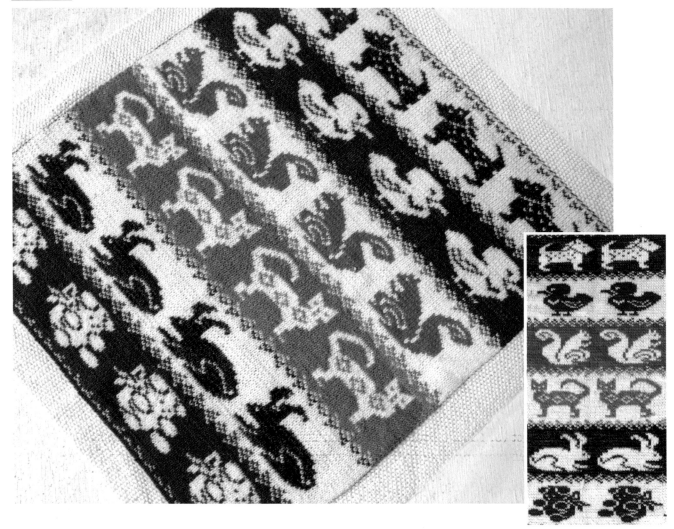

Animals from the Garden
A Baby's Blanket

This is the ideal first project for Double Knitting. Beginning with a blanket lets you understand the stitch and use up some of your many sale and left-over yarns without having to figure out how to shape a garment or sew it together. This is also an ideal gift to have around. Even though medical science is now able to tell us everything except the color of the baby's hair, we still find ourselves without the perfect gift for the newborn: especially when we would like to be able to deliver the gift the day the new family arrives home. Or better yet, the day before. So, we make yellow sweaters and green booties when we would really like to work in pink and blue.

Here is the perfect gift. Pick your colors. You may have as many as you like. You may change the size. If you find another animal you like, you may change creatures, or add to the menagerie. If you change yarn size, you can change the blanket size.

There are six rows of animals, so you can use six different colors, or two colors once and two colors twice. I chose white for the border and background so that I would have one color to carry throughout the blanket. You can make it wider by simply adding one more animal to each row, or longer by repeating a row. This blanket knits up quite quickly and the constant change of animals makes it fun for the knitter. If I become impatient, sometimes I do not knit the edging as deep as a pattern calls for. On this item you must follow directions because the depth of the bottom border should match the width of the side borders. That is the only "must". Have fun.

Finished Size: Using sport weight yarn: 28" by 30"
Using worsted weight yarn: 46" by 50"

Yarn:

Sport weight: 560 yds of white, 140 yds of each: pink, blue, yellow, and green (see notes, below).

Worsted weight: 440 yds of white, 110 yds of each: pink, blue, yellow, and green (see notes, below)

Notes on Yarn: I used washable wool for convenience since this is a baby item. Be careful when you choose a yellow. I had what I thought was a very bright yellow, but when I began knitting I found it did not contrast enough with the white and could not be seen. I had to return to the store and find a deeper gold.

Needles: For sport weight yarn, use US 5 (3.75 mm); for worsted weight, use US 8 (5 mm)

Gauge: Using sport weight yarn: 20 DSPs and 24-28 rows = 4"; using worsted weight: 16 DSPs and 20-24 rows = 4"

Directions: With color A, cast on 150 sts.

Border: Work in Seed st (or Moss st) for 2.5 in (about 20 rows). You want this border to be as tall as 15 Seed sts are wide. When working Seed stitch, always purl the last stitch on each row, and slip the first stitch knitwise. This keeps the edges even.

Next Row: In this row, you need to continue the Seed st borders (15 sts on each side), and establish Double Knitting (see Establishing DSPs, Method 2 on page 10) on the center 120 sts. Do this as follows: Using color A, sl1 knitwise, work Seed st for 14 sts. Loosely tie on color B. *Byb (both yarns back), using color A, knit the first stitch and leave it on the left-hand needle. Byf (both yarns forward), using color B, purl the same stitch and remove it from the left-hand needle. Repeat from * to last 15 sts, twist A and B yarns and, using color A only, work last 15 sts in Seed st.

Next row: Sl1 knitwise and work 14 sts in Seed st. DK (double knit) across to the last 15 sts. Twist A and B yarns and, using color A only, work last 15 sts in Seed st.

Begin Chart: Note that the 15-st borders are not shown on the chart. Work the 15 border sts, then follow the chart, repeating as indicated. Make sure to twist the two yarns at both ends of the blanket between the border and the body.

Top Border: Once you've completed the chart, you need to halve the number of stitches in the center section (all but the 15 border sts on each side). Do this as follows: Sl1 knitwise and work 14 sts in Seed st. Tie off color B, and using color A only, *k2tog, p2tog, repeat from * to last 15 sts. (Note: You are decreasing in the Seed st pattern. You may need to start decreasing with p2tog to keep your pattern in tact. Let your knitting dictate whether you start with a k2tog or p2tog.) Work last 15 sts in Seed st.

Continue in Seed st for twenty rows (or until the top border is the same size as the bottom border). Bind off.

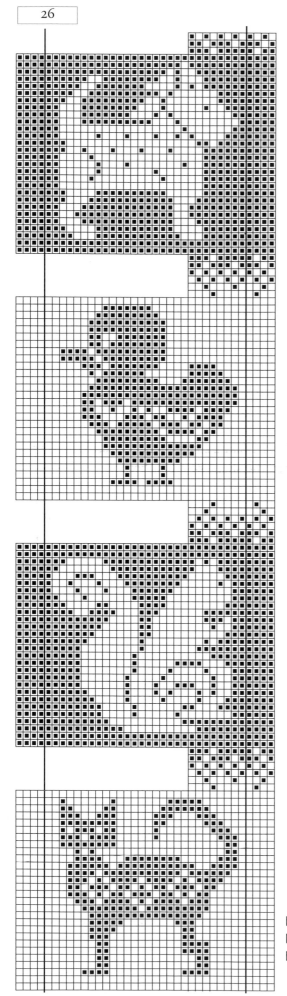

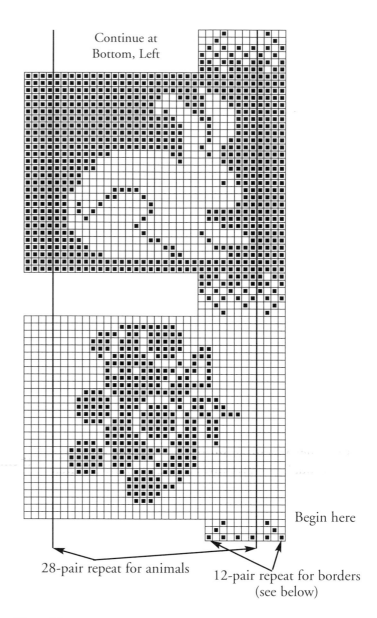

Continue at Bottom, Left

Begin here

28-pair repeat for animals

12-pair repeat for borders (see below)

Chart Notes:

1. The 15-stitch wide Seed Stitch borders are not shown on the chart.

2. When working across a row, repeat the "28-pair repeat for animals" 4 times.

3. The 6-row border pattern that separates the light and dark sections is a 12-pair repeat, as shown below as well as on the main chart.

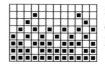

from dark to light

☐ color A on one side, color B on the other
■ color B on one side, color A on the other
☒ multiple of 10 stitches or 10 rows

from light to dark

12-pair repeat

DOUBLE KNITTING

Knitting the Refrigerator Door or, How to Keep the Children's Drawings Forever

This is a demonstration of how to chart your own project for Double Knitting. When you want to design your own work and need inspiration, you can use crochet designs, cross stitch books or any number of art books. For this project, I used a hand-drawn birthday card I had received from one of my grandchildren. Having the most beautiful and talented grandchildren in the world, I wanted to keep the picture forever. Here is how I did it.

1. I transferred the picture as accurately as possible to tracing paper. I tried to transfer directly to chart paper (graph paper) over a light box, but found what was often on the back of the drawing came through too brightly. (You know how children are kept quiet by thrusting paper and pencil at them and they draw on church bulletins, and the backs of grocery lists; I even found a drawing on the back of a wine label.)

2. I taped the tracing paper to a window (or you could use a light box) and then put graph paper over the tracing.

3. I put dots on the graph as close as possible to the drawing. I use a graph paper that has 20 squares to the inch. Use as small a graph as possible for a better knitting chart.

4. After I had a stack of drawings, I arranged them into the shape of a blanket.

For my blanket, I used worsted weight yarn and a US #5 needle. Sport weight would work as well. I began with a Moss Stitch border, kept the border going on the sides, set up for DK and when I had reached the top of the blanket, I decreased the DK stitches and finished in Moss Stitch. Complete directions for this type of blanket are in *The Animals from the Garden* on page 24.

The finished blanket was a bit wider than I like and next time I would either use sport weight yarn, or deliberately make the chart taller and not as wide. You can apply the children's names using Duplicate stitch after the blanket is finished. On my blanket, the flag that says "MOM" was actually "mother". However, "MOM" is the same on both sides, which is thrilling for a double knitter!

Once you find how much fun graphing is, you may go crazy.

DOUBLE KNITTING

Cat Bag

This bag begins with a plain base. Because there is no color pattern on the base, you can leave one side open and insert a piece of canvas or cardboard to add stability to the bottom.

Finished Size:
  Bag Width: 8"
  Bag Height: 8" before decreasing begins
  Strap Length: Your choice, sample is 22"

Gauge: 14 DSPs and 20 rows = 4"

Materials: 240 yards each of 2 colors of worsted weight yarn.

Needles: 16" circular and dp needles in US 6 (4.0 mm)

Base

Using color A, cast on 32 stitches.

Row 1: *K1, p1 in next stitch, repeat from * to end of row. This establishes DSPs (see *Establishing DSPs* on page 10). Turn.

Row 2: Loosely tie on color B, and *byb, k1 with color B, byf, p1 with color A, repeat from * to end of row. Do not twist yarns at the beginning or end of the row, creating Open Edge Stitches (OES) - see *Edge Stitches* on page 14. Turn. **Note:** Leaving the sides of the base open gives you the option of inserting a piece of canvas or cardboard to stiffen it.

Row 3: *Byb, k1 with color A, byf, p1 with color B, repeat from * to end of row. Turn.

Rows 4-15: Repeat rows 2 and 3. Turn so that side B is facing you.

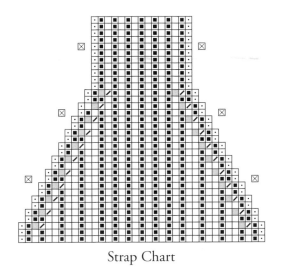

Strap Chart

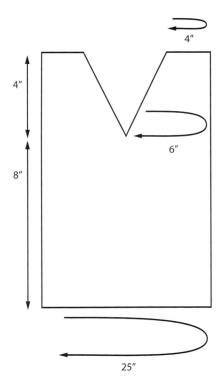

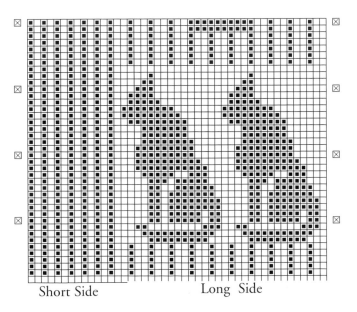

Short Side   Long Side

□ color A on front, color B on back
■ color B on front, color A on back
⊠ multiple of 10 stitches or 10 rows
· Closed Edge Stitch (CES)
▨ dec 1 DSP
⊞ inc 1 DSP

Row 16: Leave color B attached, but using color A only, *k1, p1, repeat from * across row. Turn.

Row 17: Using color A only, *k2tog, repeat from * across row. The rows of k2tog give a firm edge. You now have colors A and B ready to work.

Pick Up Around Base

I used a number of different needles when I picked up to work around the base. I started with 4 or 5 dp needles and changed to a 16" circular when it was comfortable.

Side 1 - long side
*K1 with color B, but don't remove it from left-hand needle, p1 with color A (see *Establishing DSPs* on page 10). Repeat from * in each of the 32 stitches, pm.

Side 2 - short side
*using color B, pick up one stitch from the side facing you and knit it, using color A, pick up one stitch from side farthest from you and purl it, repeat from * until you have picked up and worked 13 pairs along the short side, pm.

Side 3 - long side
Repeat Side 1.

Side 4 - short side
Repeat Side 2. Use a different colored marker at the end of this side to indicate the beginning of the round.

Body

Round 1: Begin following Body chart (begin with row 1), working in the round. The chart shows half of the bag; work each row twice.

Rounds 2-40: DK entire round following chart.

Short Row 41a, split bag for straps: Work 11 DSPs on the long side, drop color B and, using color A only, *k1, p1, repeat from * nine times more (10 pairs worked). Turn.

Short Row 41b: K2tog twice, *k1, pass previous stitch over, binding off one stitch. Repeat from * 11 times more (BO 12 total), **k2tog, pass previous stitch over, repeat from ** once more. The two single stitches of color A on each side of the BO stitches are now edge stitches (see *Edge Stitches* on page 14). The long side of bag now has 11 DSPs and one edge stitch on either side of the BO stitches. Continue: work 11 DSPs, work 13 DSPs of short side, then repeat the instructions for rows 41a and 41b on the second long side.

Row 42-62, even-numbered rows: Work back and forth on one side only, following Strap Chart: CES, DK to final stitch, CES. Turn.

Rows 43-63, odd-numbered rows: CES, work 1 DSP, dec 1 DSP, DK until 3 DSPs and edge stitch remain, dec 1 DSP, work 1 DSP, CES. Turn.

Rows 64 to desired length: CES, work 13 DSPs,

CES. I worked 32 more rows, but pause and stick it under your arm and see where strap comes on your shoulder.

Second Side

Tie on both yarns. Work back and forth as you did for the first side starting with row 42.

Finishing

Weave the two strap ends together, or sew them together with buttons, or if they are really long tie them together.

I did not want to felt the bag, but did want to fuse the fiber together, so I put it in a pillow case in the mini basket of the washer and did a gentle mini-wash. I then put it in the dryer for 5 minutes. It did not felt, but it did gain some body and I am very happy with the bag.

If you are careful to not twist the yarns on each row, you may insert a piece of canvas to give some weight and shape to the bottom. Or not. It really depends on the yarn, so I did not slip it in between the bottom layers, but cut a piece of card board when finished and simply place it in the bottom. If and when one wants to reverse the color, simple take it out and put it back.

Double Knit Bonnets

These warm helmet-type hats took some experimenting, but they were worth the trouble. The charts work for Toddler (fingering or sport weight) and Child (worsted weight) sizes. The Adult Tree design (in worsted weight) is best for adults, because of the added height.

The helmet starts with the neck ties, then is shaped with increases for a custom fit. Knit for awhile with no shaping, then decrease for the top.

Finished Size: Toddler or Child (see above)

Gauge: 20 DSPs and 28 rows = 4" in sport weight

Materials: 200 yds each of 2 colors of sport weight yarn (I like mohair) or 240 yards each of worsted weight yarn.

Needles: Circular or straight US 5 (3.75 mm)

Begin with the Ties

(See page 37 for an alternative beginning to these bonnets.)

Using color A only, cast on 79 stitches.

Row 1: Work in K1, P1 Ribbing to end of row. Turn.

Row 2: Repeat row 1.

Row 3: Work 3 stitches in ribbing, BO 2 stitches (buttonhole), work ribbing to end of row. Turn.

Row 4: Work in ribbing to buttonhole, CO 2 stitches, rib to end of row. Turn.

Row 5 & 6: Repeat row 1.

Row 7: Bind off 10 stitches in ribbing, work ribbing to end of row.

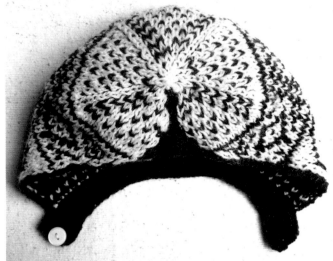

Row 8: Bind off 8 stitches in ribbing, k3 (to begin Garter Stitch edging). Loosely tie on color B and establish DSPs as follows: *Byb (both yarns back), using A, knit the first stitch and leave it on the left-hand needle, byf (both yarns forward), using B, purl the same stitch and remove it from the left-hand needle (see *Establishing DSPs* on page 10). Repeat from * until 4 stitches remain, using color A only, k4.

Note: For the rest of this pattern, GS4 means:

- at the beginning of each row, k4 stitches, then twist colors A and B around each other to prevent a hole.

- at the end of each row, when 4 stitches remain, using color A only, k4.

□	color A on one side, color B on the other
▣	color B on one side, color A on the other
⊠	multiple of 10 stitches or 10 rows
▱⧄	dec 1 DSP
⊞	inc 1 DSP
⊞	change single stitch into DSP

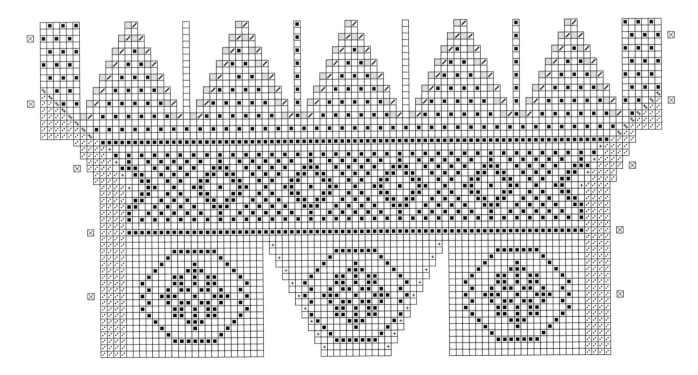

DOUBLE KNITTING

☐ color A on one side, color B on the other
■ color B on one side, color A on the other
⊠ multiple of 10 stitches or 10 rows
▱◪ dec 1 DSP
⊞ inc 1 DSP
⊕ change single stitch into DSP

DOUBLE KNITTING

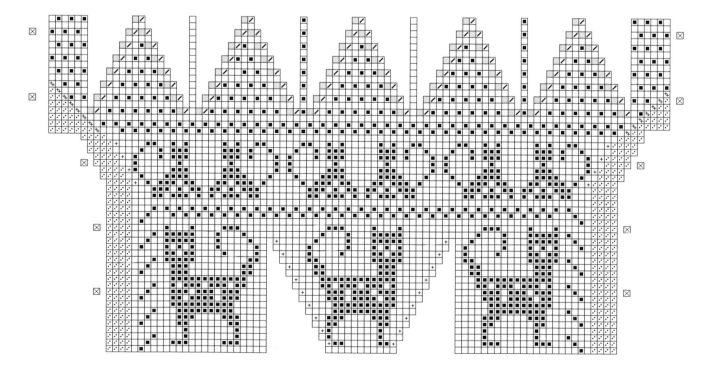

Bonnet

You now have 53 pairs for DK pattern, and 4 Garter Stitches on each edge.

Row 1: GS4, DK to end of row following chart, GS4.

Row 2: GS4, DK 21 pairs following chart. Put a marker on the needle. Inc 1 DSP, work 11 pairs, inc 1 DSP, pm, work 21 pairs, GS4.

Rows 3-34: DK as established, increasing where shown on chart.

Crown

Row 35: GS2, change next stitch into DSP, work 81 DSPs, change next stitch into DSP, GS2, cast on 5. Turn.

Row 36: GS6, change next stitch into DSP, work 83 DSPs, change next stitch into DSP, GS1, cast on 4. Turn.

Row 37: GS5, change next stitch into DSP, work 85 DSPs, change next stitch into DSP, GS5. Turn.

Rows 38-52: Continue as established, changing single stitches into DSPs and decreasing where indicated on chart - 21 pairs remain.

Finishing

Break off yarns, leaving a 10-12 inch tail. Use the tail of color A to weave (Kitchener) the first 6 color A stitches to the last 6 color A stitches; this joins the hat at the back of the head. Turn hat inside out and use the tail of color B to weave together the first and last 6 color B stitches. Run the color A tail through the 9 remaining color A stitches, repeat for color B. Pull the strands tight to gather stitches. Weave in ends. The lower photo on page 34 shows the back of the bonnet.

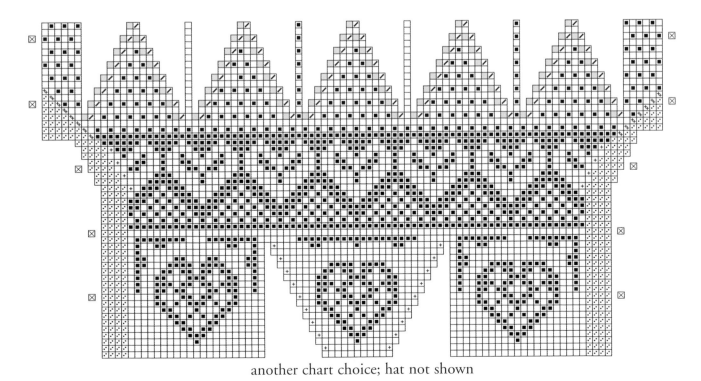

another chart choice; hat not shown

DOUBLE KNITTING

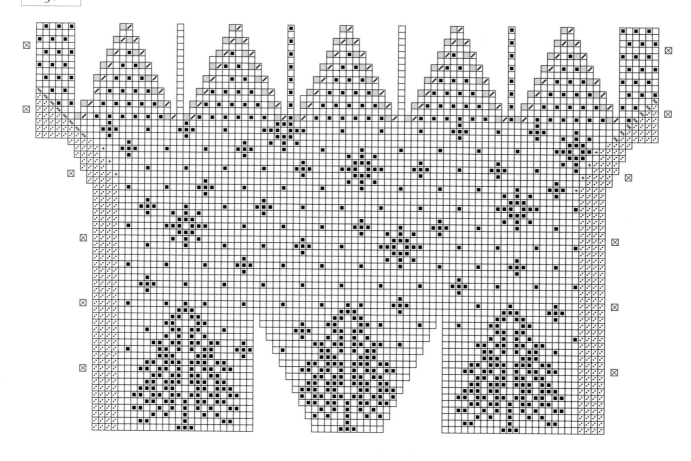

Adult-size chart; added height

□ color A on one side, color B on the other
■ color B on one side, color A on the other
⊠ multiple of 10 stitches or 10 rows
▨ dec 1 DSP
⊞ inc 1 DSP
⊕ change single stitch into DSP

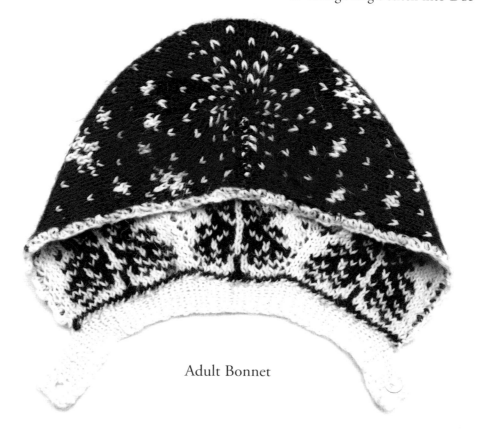

Adult Bonnet

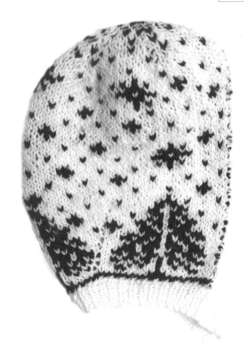

Adult Bonnet

Sew two buttons on the band, one on each side to maintain reversibility. The crown goes together so smoothly there is no need for a pom-pon. This helmet is especially good for windy weather.

Alternate Beginning to Bonnets

Using color A only, CO 125 stitches.

Row 1-6: Work in k1, p1 ribbing.

Row 7: BO 32 stitches loosely in ribbing, rib to end.

Row 8: BO 32 stitches loosely in ribbing, rib to end - 61 stitches remain.

Rows 9-11: Work in k1, p1 ribbing.

Row 12: Still using color A, work 5 stitches in ribbing, tie on B and establish DSPs (see *Establishing DSPs* on page 10) until 5 stitches remain, twist the 2 yarns to avoid a hole, using color A only, work 5 stitches in ribbing. You now have 5 ribbing stitches, 53 DSPs and 5 ribbing stitches.

Follow instructions and charts for the hat of your choice, but work 5 ribbing stitches at each edge instead of the 4 Garter Stitches.

Camilla
A Fair Isle Vest

This vest is simple, short and casual. It does not button, so is a great first garment project. The vest is knit from the bottom up to the armholes and then divided: each front and the back are worked separately. The shoulders are then woven together separately to keep the vest completely reversible.

To make a larger vest, increase the stitches down the middle of the back and under each arm, or use a larger yarn and needles. I used five colors and they really were scraps. This would be a good project to use any or as many colors as you like. I began with a dark brown, but did not use brown in every row. To unify the vest, I applied I-cord around all edges.

I used brown, orange, gold, blue and gray. I used two colors in each motif and then carried one of those colors to the next motif and introduced a third color. On the third motif I used the second color and introduced the fourth color and so on. I then repeated my color pattern, but you could use different colors every time.

Finished Size: 35" circumference

Gauge: 20 DSPs and 30 rows for 4"

Materials: 150 yds each of sport weight yarn in colors: brown, orange, gold, blue, and grey. (I used Shetland Jumper Weight wool.

Needles: 24" US 4 (3.5mm) circular needle, US 4 dp needles

Body

Using 2 strands of color A held together, cast on 175 stitches (see *Casting On* on page 10). This immediately gives you DSPs. Turn.

Row 1: Cut off one strand of color A, sl 1 p'wise, loosely tie on color B, and *byb, k1 with color A, byf, p1 with color B, repeat from * to last stitch, twist the two colors and, using color A only, k1. Turn.

Note: For the rest of this pattern, CES (Closed Edge Stitch) means:
  - at the beginning of each row, sl 1 single stitch p'wise, pick up color B and twist yarns to prevent hole, continue.
  - at the end of each row, drop color B on the side of your work closest to you and, using color A only, knit the last single stitch.

Row 2: Begin following chart (start on row 2) CES, DK to last stitch, CES. Turn.

Rows 3-60: Work as established, decreasing as shown on chart.

(continues on page 42)

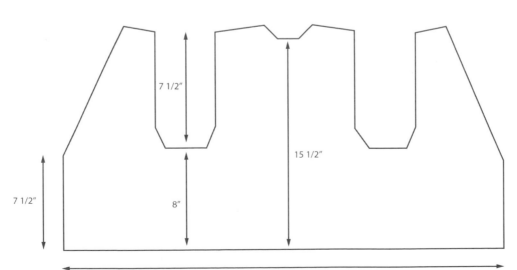

Camilla Fair Isle Vest chart

Pivot Stitch

DOUBLE KNITTING

☐ color A on one side, color B on the other
▣ color B on one side, color A on the other
⊠ multiple of 10 stitches or 10 rows
⊡ Closed Edge Stitch (CES)
▱✓ dec 1 DSP

Legend for the **Camilla Vest** chart

Row 61, armhole: CES, work 39 DSPs, *byb, using color A only, knit together the 2 stitches that make up the next pair (to establish edge stitch for armhole), BO 11 DSPs, byb, using color A only, knit together the next pair**, work 63 DSPs, repeat from * to **, work 39 DSPs, k1. Turn.

Left Front

Row 62-114: Work as established following chart.

Row 115, shoulder shaping: CES, DK 8 pairs, dec 1 DSP, work to last stitch, CES. Turn.

Row 116: CES, work 7 DSPs, dec 1 DSP, work 1 pair, turn.

Row 117: CES, work 9 DSPs, put 18 DSPs and 2 edge stitches on hold.

Right Front

Row 62: Starting at armhole edge, reattach colors A and B. Keep both edges as CESs and DK to end of row.

Work exactly as you did for Left Front.

Back

Row 62: Reattach colors A and B. Keep both edges as CESs and DK to end of row.

Rows 63-115: Continue as established following chart.

Row 116: CES, DK 17 pairs, dec 1 DSP, CES. Turn.

Row 117, first shoulder: CES, dec 1 DSP, DK 8 pairs. Turn.

Row 118: DK 9 pairs, CES. Put 18 DSPs and 2 edge stitches on hold.

Second Shoulder

Row 117: Starting at armhole edge, join in color A. Work exactly as you did for first shoulder, above.

Finishing

*Take the stitches for the front right shoulder and split them onto two needles as follows: edge stitches and color A stitches on one needle, color B stitches on the second needle. Repeat this process for the right shoulder stitches from the back of the vest. Using color A, either kitchener the color A shoulder stitches together, or use 3-needle BO to unite them. Turn to the other side and repeat with color B stitches. Repeat from * for left shoulder stitches.

Use a sewing needle or crochet hook to work any loose ends into the fabric. Apply I-cord around the entire vest (see EZ's *Applied I-Cord* on page 15).

Mary, Mary, Quite Contrary
A Flower Shawl

This shawl is worked from the bottom to the back neck and then divided into two wings. I finished mine with a crocheted edge. I-cord would also be nice. While finishing, I added a button loop on each wing and then tried it on to position my buttons. I found two very nice antique buttons in a thrift shop.

The border is Seed or Moss Stitch - your choice (see page 16); and the body is done in Double Knitting. You work the chart to center back, work the Pivot Stitch, then work back to the right edge of the chart (see *Reading Charts* on page 17).

Finished Size: see schematic on page 49

Materials: Fingering weight yarn, 1650 yards of each color. I used Hanake Merino yarn.

Gauge: 20 DSPs and 32 rows = 4"

Needles: 24" US #4 circular

Notions: Crochet hook, 2 buttons

Border: The border is worked in Seed or Moss Stitch. When working the border, knit the last stitch on each row, and slip the first stitch p'wise. This keeps the edges even.

Begin Shawl

Using color A, cast on 47 stitches.

Edge Stitch (ES): Always slip the first stitch p'wise, and always knit the last stitch.

Rows 1-12: ES, inc 1 stitch, work border stitch (Moss or Seed) to within 1 stitch of end, inc 1 stitch, ES (71 stitches).

Row 13: In this row, continue increasing the borders and establish Double Knitting (see *Establishing DSPs* on page 10) on the center 53 stitches. Do this as follows: ES, inc in next stitch, work border stitch for 8 stitches, pm, k and p into each of the next 53 stitches, pm, work 8 stitches in border stitch, inc in next stitch, ES. You now have 10 border stitches, 53 DSPs, 10 border stitches).

Row 14: ES, work border stitch for 9 stitches, loosely tie on color B, *byb, k1 with color B, byf, p1 with color A, repeat from * until second marker, drop color B on the side closest to you (so that it is in position for the next row), work 9 stitches in border stitch, ES.

Note: For the rest of this pattern, **Border** means:
  - at the beginning of the row: Using color A only, sl 1 p'wise, work 9 stitches in border stitch, add in color B, twist the two yarns to avoid a hole where the border meets the Double Knitting.
  - at the end of the row: drop color B on the side closest to you, using color A only, work 9 stitches in border stitch, k1.

Row 15: Begin following the chart (begin with row 15). See *Reading Charts* on page 17 for details on following a chart in Double Knitting. From here onward, the increases are done in the DK section, but not the borders (see *Increasing a DSP* on page 11). Work across the chart from right to left. After you work the Pivot Stitch, reverse the chart to complete the row, but only work the Pivot Stitch once.

Rows 16-249: Continue as established, increasing where indicated on chart.

The rest of this pattern assumes that you are doing both wings at the same time. You may opt to finish the right wing, then finish the left afterwards.

Row 250, prepare for back of neck: Border, DK 117 pairs, pm, drop color B, using color A only, k1, p1 across 55 pairs (110 stitches), pm, loosely tie on another strand of color B and continue to DK to next marker, Border.

Row 251-259: Work as established, following chart.

Row 260, back of neck: Border, DK to next marker, work 8 stitches in border stitch, k1, BO 47 stitches in border stitch, sl 1, work 8 stitches in border stitch, DK to next marker, Border.

Note: For this row only, the neck border has 9 stitches instead of 10.

Rows 261-390: Continue as established, following chart.

Note: Row 265 is the last row with increases at the outer edges.

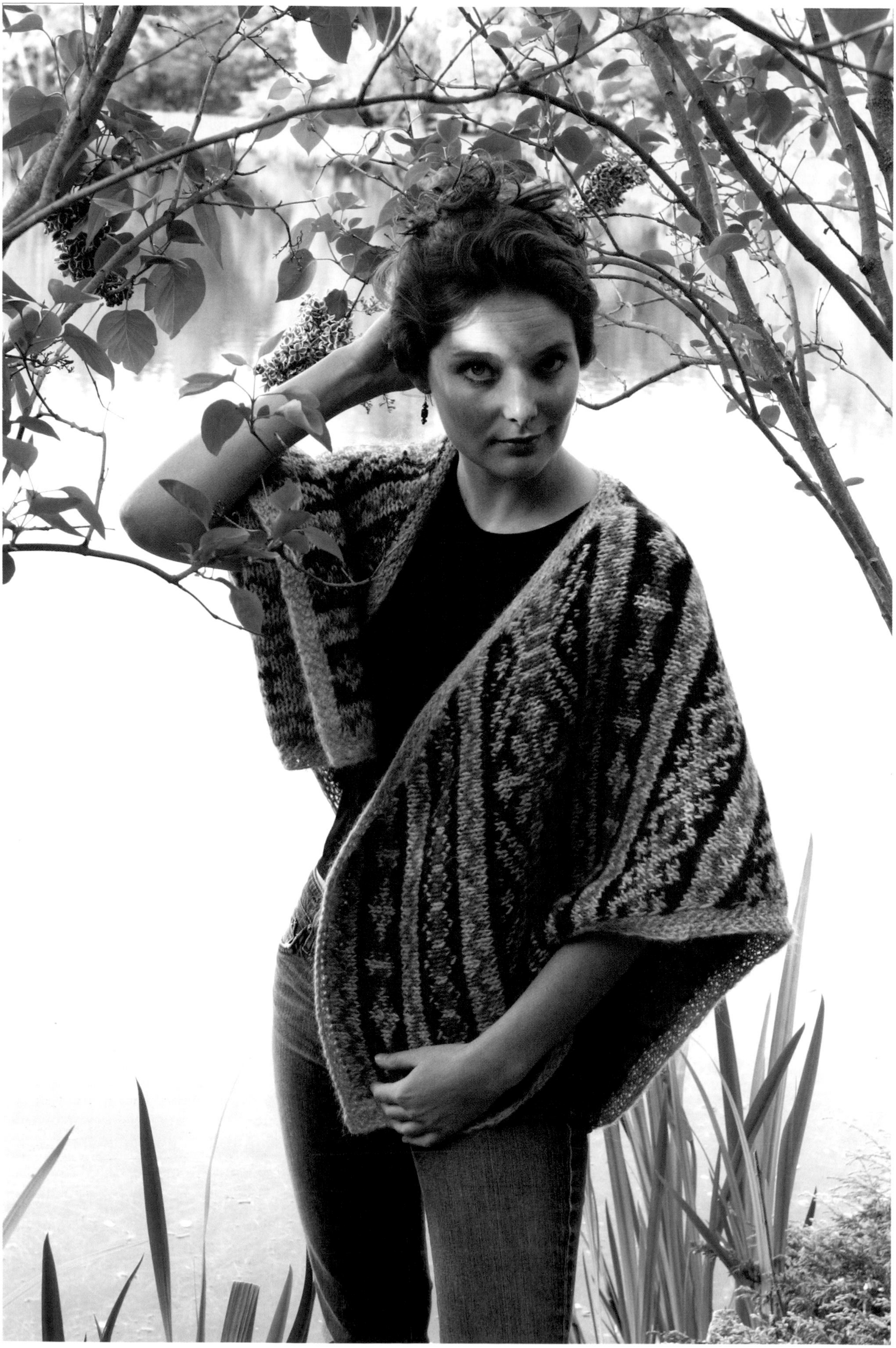

The Highlands
A Fair Isle Shawl

Here is something made simply in one piece with no seams. This lovely shawl uses five colors. They do not have to be the colors I have listed, but can be your favorites. The shawl is knit from the bottom up to the back of the neck, then the two wings are knit separately. It begins with Moss Stitch and has Moss Stitch on all the edges. When worn, the wings fold across the chest nicely and the shawl actually stays on without any pinning. However, I often hold it in place with a Shawl Clasp.

Finished Size: See schematic on page 53.

Border: 5 stitches on all sides in Moss Stitch.

Yarn: Worsted weight: 660 yds of natural, 220 yds of each: dark red, medium red, orange, and green. The sample was knitted using Reynolds Lopi Light (110 yds per skein).

Needles: 24" US 8 (5 mm) circular

Gauge: 13 DSPs and 18 rows = 4"

Begin Shawl

With color A, cast on 23 stitches.

Row 1: *K1, p1, repeat from * to last stitch, k first row of Moss Stitch.

Row 2: Sl 1 p'wise, inc 1 stitch. Work Moss Stitch to last stitch, inc l in pattern, k1 (25 stitches).

Rows 3-6: Repeat row 2 (33 stitches).

Row 7: In this row, continue increasing the borders, and establish Double Knitting (see *Establishing DSPs,* on page 10) on the center 25 stitches. Do this as follows: Still using color A only, sl 1 p'wise, inc in next stitch, work Moss Stitch for 3 stitches, pm, k and p into each of the next 25 stitches, pm, work 3 stitches in Moss Stitch, inc in next stitch, k1. You now have 5 border stitches, 25 DSPs, 5 border stitches.

Row 8: Begin following chart (start with row 8 (see *Reading Charts* on page 17 for details on following a chart in Double Knitting). Work this row as follows: Sl 1 p'wise, work 4 stitches in Moss Stitch, loosely tie on color B, and DK across to the Pivot Stitch on chart, then reverse the chart (only work the Pivot Stitch once) and work from left to right until second marker, drop color B on the side closest to you and, using color A only, work 4 stitches in Moss, k1.

Note: For the rest of this pattern, **Border** means:
- at the beginning of the row: Using color A only, sl 1 p'wise, work 4 stitches in Moss Stitch, add in color B, twist the two yarns to avoid a hole where the border meets the Double Knitting.
- at the end of the row: drop color B on the side closest to you, using color A only, work 4 stitches in Moss Stitch, k1.

From here on, the increases are done in the DK section, not the borders.

Rows 9-126: Continue as established, increasing where indicated on chart (see *Increasing DSPs* on page 11).

Row 127: prepare for back of neck: Border, inc 1 DSP, DK 57 pairs, pm, drop color B, and using color A only, k1, p1 across 29 pairs (58 stitches), pm, loosely tie in another strand of color B and continue to DK to next marker, Border.

Row 128: Border, DK to next marker, using color A only, k2tog, p2tog to next marker, DK to next marker, Border.

Row 129: Border, DK to within 2 pairs of next marker, dec 1 DSP (see *Decreasing DSPs* on page 13), work 29 stitches in Moss Stitch, dec 1 DSP, DK to next marker, Border.

Row 130: Border, DK to next marker, work 31 stitches in Moss Stitch, DK to next marker, Border.

Row 131, back of neck: Border, inc 1 DSP, DK to next marker, work 4 stitches in Moss Stitch, k1, BO 23 stitches in Moss Stitch, sl 1, work 4 stitches in Moss Stitch, DK 58 pairs, inc 1 DSP, Border.

You now have 2 wings: I worked both sides at the same time, but if this is too much yarn hanging about, finish one wing and then work the other.

Wings

Row 132-193: Continue as established, increasing and decreasing as shown on chart and working both wings.

Row 194: Using color A only, Border, k2tog, p2tog across to next marker, Border. (**Note:** You may need to start with p2tog to keep the Moss Stitch pattern intact. Let your knitting dictate whether you start with a k2tog or p2tog.) Repeat for second wing.

Row 195-197: Work in Moss Stitch. Repeat for second wing.

BO all stitches in Moss Stitch.

Second Wing (if not worked simultaneously)

If you decided to finish the 2 wings separately, start with row 132 and work second wing.

Finishing

Use a sewing needle or crochet hook to work any loose ends into the fabric. Buy a pretty brooch.

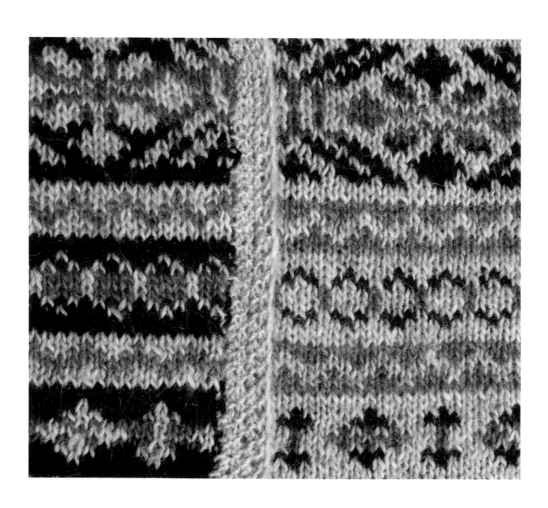

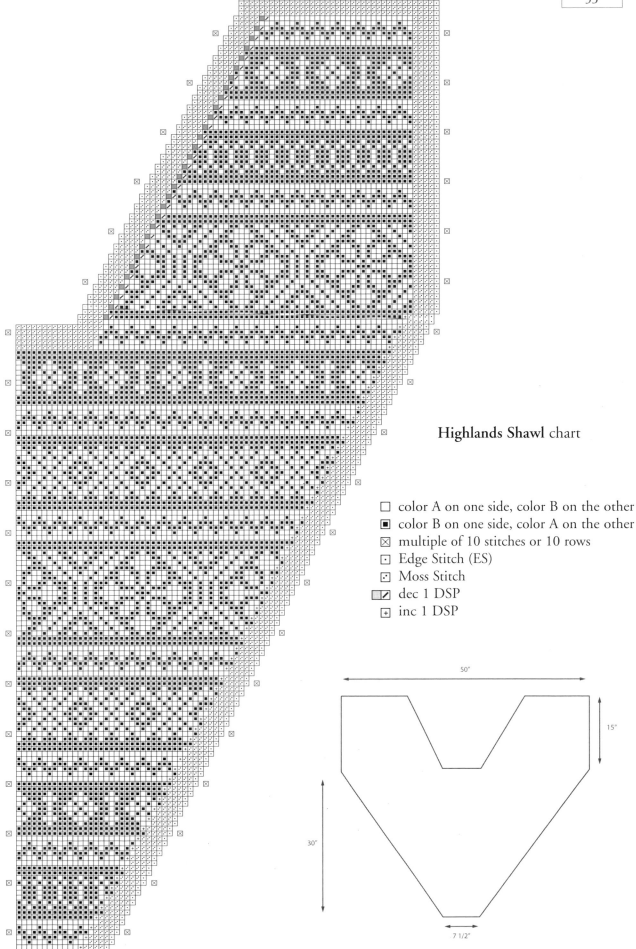

Highlands Shawl chart

☐ color A on one side, color B on the other
■ color B on one side, color A on the other
⊠ multiple of 10 stitches or 10 rows
⊡ Edge Stitch (ES)
⊡ Moss Stitch
◪ dec 1 DSP
⊞ inc 1 DSP

50"

15"

30"

7 1/2"

DOUBLE KNITTING

Moorish Tiles
A Top-Down Child's Cardigan

My aim with this sweater was to have as few seams as possible, so I designed a cardigan I could knit from the neck down and use either straight or circular needles. The sweater is worked back and forth from one front to the other. I started with straight needles and switched to circular when I could not hold any more stitches on the straight needles.

Finished Size:

Size **2** (4, 6, 8, 10, 12)

Materials: 50 gram skeins of sport weight yarn, approximately 110 yards each:

Color A: **3** (3,3,4,4,4) 50 gram skeins,
Color B: **3** (3,3,4,4,4) 50 gram skeins,
12 buttons

Needles: US 6 (4 mm) straight and 24" circular

Gauge: 20 DSPs and 22 rows = 4"

Body

Using 24" circular needle and color A, CO **23** (25, 31, 33, 33, 35) stitches.

Note: The charts show the shaping for size 2; for the other sizes, follow the numbers in the written instructions and use the charts as a guide.

Set-Up Row: Loosely tie on color B and establish Double Knitting as follows: *Byb (both yarns back), using color B, knit the first stitch and leave it on the left-hand needle (see *Establishing DSPs* on page 10), byf (both yarns forward), using color A, purl the same stitch and remove it from the left-hand needle. Repeat from * to end of row. This turns each stitch of the foundation row into a DSP (Double-Stitch Pair).

Row 1: Begin following chart (start with row 1), and place markers for size you are making as follows:

Size 2: 2 pairs for front, pm, 2 pairs for sleeve, pm, 15 pairs for back, pm, 2 pairs for sleeve, pm, 2 pairs for front.

Size 4: 2 pairs for front, pm, 2 pairs for sleeve, pm, 17 pairs for back, pm, 2 pairs for sleeve, pm, 2 pairs for front.

Size 6: 2 pairs for front, pm, 4 pairs for sleeve, pm, 19 pairs for back, pm, 4 pairs for sleeve, pm, 2 pairs for front.

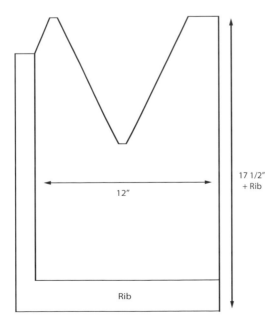

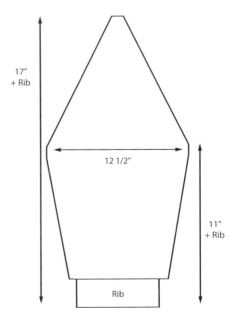

DOUBLE KNITTING

For the hat, see Double Knit Bonnets on page 32

Size 8: 2 pairs for front, pm, 4 pairs for sleeve, pm, 21 pairs for back, pm, 4 pairs for sleeve, pm, 2 pairs for front.

Size 10: 2 pairs for front, pm, 4 pairs for sleeve, pm, 21 pairs for back, pm, 4 pairs for sleeve, pm, 2 pairs for front.

Size 12: 2 pairs for front, pm, 4 pairs for sleeve, pm, 23 pairs for back, pm, 4 pairs for sleeve, pm, 2 pairs for front.

Work from right to left across front chart, sleeve chart, back chart to Pivot Stitch (see *Pivot Stitch* on page 17), then reverse the chart and work from left to right across back chart again, sleeve chart, then front chart. Turn.

Row 2, raglan increase: Work across charts as established, and inc 1 DSP on both sides of each marker. This adds 8 pairs. Turn.

Row 3, increase at front edges: Work 1 DSP, inc 1 DSP, DK following charts until 1 pair remains, inc 1 DSP, work final pair. Turn.

Rows 4-11: For sizes 2, 4, and 6, repeat the shaping described in rows 2 and 3 four times more. For sizes 8, 10, and 12, repeat the shaping described in rows 2 and 3 five times more.

Row 12: Work across charts as established, and inc 1 DSP on both sides of each marker.

Row 13: increase at front edge and CO front band: Work 1 DSP, inc 1 DSP, DK following charts until 1 pair remains, inc 1 DSP, work final pair. At end of row, pm, using color A only, CO 8 stitches. Turn.

Row 14: raglan increase and CO front band: Slip 1 single stitch p'wise, work 7 stitches in k1, p1 ribbing. Pick up color B and twist the two yarns together to avoid a hole. Work across charts as established, and inc 1 DSP on both sides of each marker. At end of row, pm, using color A only, CO 8 stitches. Turn.

Note: For the rest of this pattern, FB (Front Band) means:
 - at the beginning of each row, sl 1 p'wise, work 7 stitches in k1, p1 ribbing, twist colors A and B to avoid a hole where the band meets the Double Knitting.
 - at the end of each row, drop color B on the side of the work closest to you and, using color A only, work 7 stitches in k1, p1 ribbing, k1.

Row 15: FB, DK as established until marker before second edge, FB.

Row 16: FB, work across charts as established increasing 1 DSP on both sides of each marker, FB.

Continue: Repeat shaping as described in rows 15 and 16 until you have worked **23** (25, 26, 28, 30, 32) raglan increases, and place buttonholes every 2-3 inches along the Front Bands (see below). You now have: 8 Front Band stitches and **31** (33, 34, 36, 38, 40) pairs for each front section, 48 (52,

56, 60, 64, 68) pairs for each sleeve, and **61** (67, 71, 77, 81, 87) pairs for the back.

Buttonholes: To work a buttonhole, slip the first stitch, work 2 stitches in ribbing, BO two stitches, then work the final 3 stitches of the Front Band in ribbing. On the next row, cast on 2 stitches in place of the two bound off stitches, and continue.

Next Row: FB, work across front stitches, place sleeve stitches on a piece of yarn as a holder, DK across the back DSPs, put the second sleeve on hold, work across front section, FB. You now have the two sets of Front Band stitches, and **123** (133, 139, 149, 157, 167) pairs for the body.

Continue: Keeping Front Bands as established, continue working on the body of the sweater only. Work until the piece measures **8"** (8", 9", 10", 10", 11") from the point where you put the sleeves on hold.

Next Row, decrease to one color: FB, * byb, k1 with color B, byf, p1 with color A, pass the color B loop over the color A loop. Repeat from * to next band, FB.

Bottom Ribbing: Tie off color B and, using color A only, work 2"-3" in k1, p1 ribbing. Bind off loosely in ribbing.

Sleeves

Move the stitches for one sleeve back to your working needles. Loosely tie on both colors at the edge. Work the sleeves flat, keeping Open Edge Stitches (OESs, see *Edge Stitches* on page 14); this lets you sew the sleeve seams together when finished, each side separately.

Continue: Work sleeves following chart, decreasing every 6 rows 4 (6, 8, 9, 10, 11) times. Work straight on **40**, (40, 40, 42, 44, 46) stitches until piece measures **6"** (7", 9", 9", 10", 11") inches from underarm.
Next Row, decrease to one color: * Byb, k1 with color B, byf, p1 with color A, pass the color B loop over the color A loop. Repeat from * to end of row.

Next Row: Work in k1, p1 ribbing across row, decreasing 6 (8, 8, 10, 10, 12) stitches evenly spaced.

Work in k1, p1 ribbing for 2", bind off in ribbing.

Neckband

Using color A, knit up (see *Pick Up vs Knit Up* on page 16) about **65** (67, 71, 73, 77, 79) stitches. Work in k1, p1 ribbing for 1.5", adding another buttonhole. Bind off loosely in ribbing.

Finishing

Sew sleeve seams separately (side A to side A, then side B to side B). Sew sleeves into armholes the same way. Sew buttons on both sides.

DK - Geometric
White + grape

Nordic Summer
A Lovely Cardigan for a Child

Is there a knitter among us who did not become enchanted with the Nordic sweaters seen on television during the Winter Olympics in Norway? Here is a sweater and hat design as my tribute to the Vikings.

This child's sweater and hat and will fit sizes 2 to 6, depending on the usual child stuff of weight and height. It is knit in one piece from the bottom ribbing to the armholes, including the buttonhole band. A few stitches are cast off for the armhole and then the body of the sweater is knit with three separate pieces, the two fronts and the back. Since it is a child's sweater it knits up rather fast. This sweater takes twice as many buttons as the normal cardigan because they are sewn on both sides.

Finished Size:
Size: 2, 4, 6
Finished chest: 23", 25", 27"
Upper sleeve: 11", 12", 12"

Materials: 500 (600-700) yards each of two colors sport weight yarn.

Gauge: 24 DSPs and 24 rows = 4"

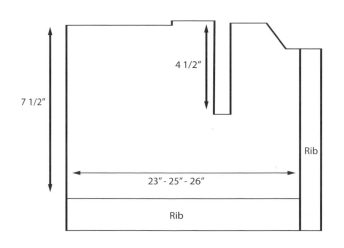

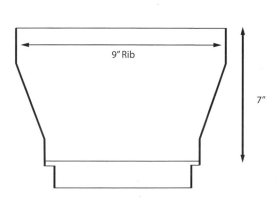

7 1/2"

4 1/2"

23" - 25" - 26"

Rib

Rib

9" Rib

7"

Needles: 24" circular, straight and dpns in size US 3 (3.0 mm) and dpns in US 1 (1.5 mm)

Notions: Stitch holders, tapestry needle, fourteen buttons

Body

Using smaller needles and color A (or B, if you choose that for the ribbing color), CO 137 (149, 161) stitches.

Rows 1-12: Sl 1 p'wise, work in k1, p1 ribbing until 1 stitch remains, k1. Turn.

Note: Work buttonhole on row 4 as shown on chart.

Row 13: Change to larger needles, sl 1 p'wise, work in k1, p1 ribbing for 7 stitches, pm, loosely tie on color B and establish DSPs as follows (see *Establishing DSPs* on page 10): *byb, k1 with color

B, byf, p1 with color A, repeat from * until 8 stitches remain, pm, work 7 stitches in k1, p1 ribbing, k1. Turn. You now have 8 front band stitches, 121 (133, 145) DSPs, and 8 front band stitches.

Note: For the rest of this pattern, FB (Front Band) means:

 - at the beginning of each row, sl 1 p'wise, work 7 stitches in k1, p1 ribbing. Pick up second color, twist colors A and B to avoid a hole where the band meets the Double Knitting, start working DK.

 - at the end of each row when 8 stitches remain, drop non-border color on the side of your work closest to you and, using border color only, work 7 stitches in k1, p1 ribbing, k1.

Row 14: Begin following body chart (start with row 14). FB, DK to next marker, FB. **Note:** Read the chart from right to left until you get to the Pivot Stitch for the size you are making (see

Reading Charts on page 17), then work across the same row from left to right (work Pivot Stitch only once).

Rows 15-42: FB, DK to next marker, FB. Work buttonhole on rows 16, 28, and 40 as shown on chart.

Note: Measure the sweater before working row 43 and adjust length if needed. If you make the sweater longer, the row numbers in this pattern will be different than yours. Keep in mind that you want to place a buttonhole about every 12 rows.

Row 43: armholes: Following chart for the size you are making: Front Band, work 27 (30, 33) DSPs, BO sep 6 DSPs, work 56 (60, 66) DSPs, BO sep 6 DSPs, work 26 (29, 32) DSPs, FB.

Note: The final two stitches from each of the bound-off sections are added to the count, so you now have 27 (30, 33) DSPs (plus front bands) for each front section and 57 (61, 67) DSPs for the back. Leave the back and one front section on the circular needle, and continue on one front section only.

First Front

Rows 44-66: Work on one front section only and follow chart for the size you are making: FB, DK to armhole edge. Turn. Keep an Open Edge Stitch (OES - see *Edge Stitches* on page 14) at the armhole edge to help keep the seams reversible. **Note:** Work buttonhole on rows 52 and 64 as shown on chart (or every 12th row, if you adjusted length). I suggest working 2" (2.5", 3") above armhole before beginning the flower pattern.

Row 67: neck shaping: The neck shaping is the same for all sizes: FB, work 5 DSPs. Slip all of these stitches to a holder. DK to end of row. Turn.

Row 68: DK to new front edge (ignoring stitches on holder). Turn.

Row 69: DK 2 pairs and move them to the same holder, DK to end of row. Turn.

Rows 70-76: Follow chart as established, adding stitches to holder as shown on chart. Turn.

BO sep all stitches.

Second Front

Tie on both colors at the front edge and work exactly as you did for First Front.

Back

Tie on both colors.

Row 44-74: Keeping an OES on both edges, follow chart. Turn.

Note: If you made the fronts longer, don't forget to make the back longer too.

DK or fingering
flowers & pots
red & white

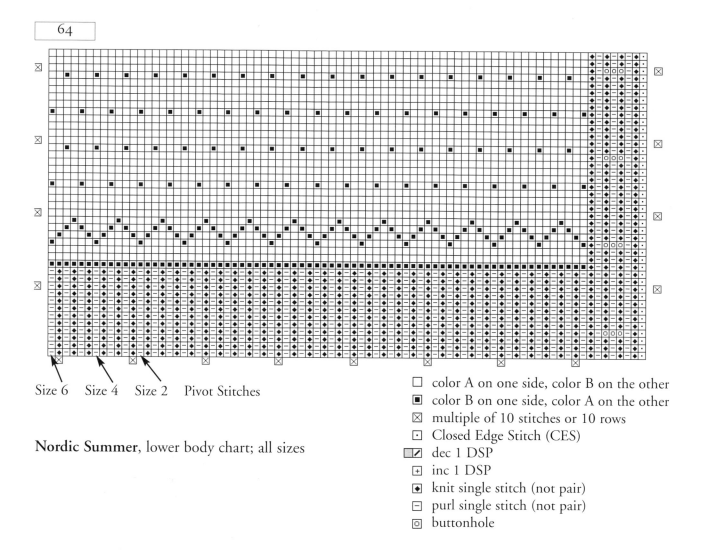

Size 6   Size 4   Size 2   Pivot Stitches

Nordic Summer, lower body chart; all sizes

☐ color A on one side, color B on the other
■ color B on one side, color A on the other
☒ multiple of 10 stitches or 10 rows
· Closed Edge Stitch (CES)
◩ dec 1 DSP
⊞ inc 1 DSP
◆ knit single stitch (not pair)
⊟ purl single stitch (not pair)
▣ buttonhole

Row 75: neck shaping: Work 14 (17, 20) DSPs. Using ribbing color, *k2tog, repeat from * 27 times (you can either carry the second color along, or add in a new piece on the other side of the neck). After working those 27 stitches, move them to a holder, DK to end of row. Turn.

Row 76: first shoulder: DK 14 (17, 20) pairs. Turn.

BO sep all stitches.

Repeat row 76 and BO for second shoulder.

Shoulder Seams

Using color A, weave or sew together the color A shoulders. Turn to the other side and weave or sew the color B stitches.

Neck Band

Note: I know most directions say, "pick up and knit", but in Double Knitting I like to pick up in knit and purl. I think it looks better, and on this type of garment, it is especially important to not have one side look like the "wrong" side.

Row 1: Starting at either side of the neck, move the stitches from one holder to the smaller circular needle. Join the ribbing color and work Front Band. Now you need to change to k1, p1 ribbing, add stitches, and incorporate all stitches from holders as follows: K2tog, p2tog, k2tog, p2tog, k2tog, m1, k2tog, p2tog, m1, p2tog, k2tog, m1, k2tog, p2tog, m1, p2tog, k2tog. Pick up and rib 5 stitches across shoulder to the back of the neck.

Put the 27 pairs from the back neck onto a needle, and work *k2tog, p2tog, repeat from * across those 27 pairs.

DOUBLE KNITTING

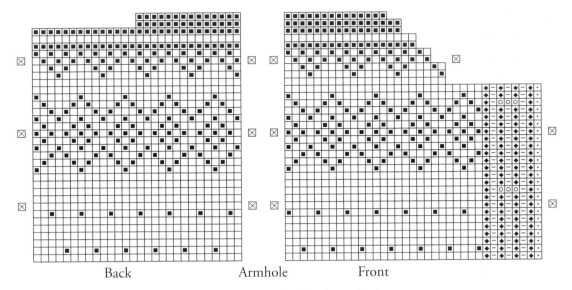

Back   Armhole   Front

Nordic Summer upper body chart for **Size 2**

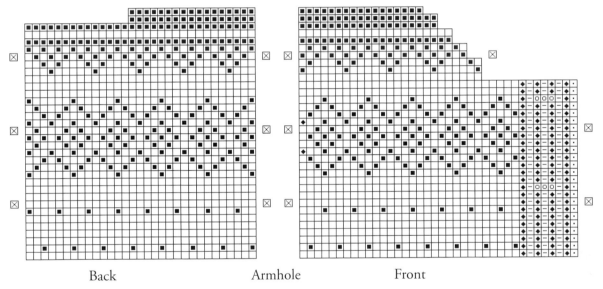

Back   Armhole   Front

Nordic Summer upper body chart for **Size 4**

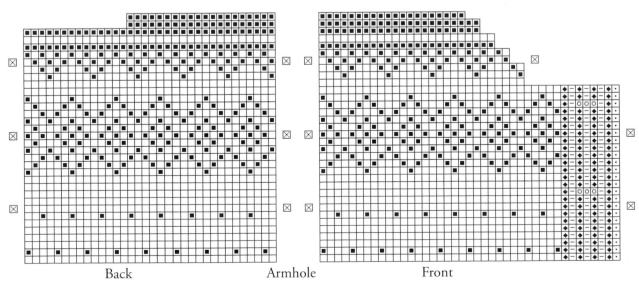

Back   Armhole   Front

Nordic Summer upper body chart for **Size 6**

DOUBLE KNITTING

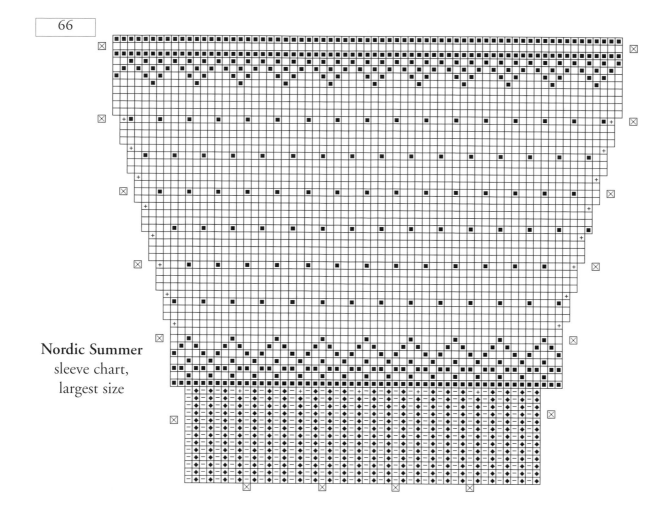

Nordic Summer
sleeve chart,
largest size

Pick up and rib 5 stitches across shoulder, then move the stitches from the other front holder to a needle. K2tog, p2tog, m1, p2tog, k2tog, m1, k2tog, p2tog, m1, p2tog, k2tog, m1, k2tog, p2tog, k2tog, p2tog, k2tog, FB. Turn.

Rows 2 to 14 (or your choice): Work in k1, p1 ribbing for a half inch, work one last buttonhole, then work at least 3 or 4 more rows.

BO loosely in rib.

Sleeves

I made the sleeves flat and sewed the underarm seams; if you don't mind working on dp needles, or two circulars, you can certainly work them in the round.

Using smaller needles and ribbing color, CO 44 (46-48) stitches.

Ribbing: Work in kl, pl ribbing for about 1.5 inches - the ribbing is not shown on the chart.

Next Row: Work in ribbing, but increase 5 stitches evenly spaced (49, 51, 53).

DK Set-Up Row: Change to larger needles and attach color B. Establish DSPs across the entire row as you did for the body. If working flat, keep an OES on both sides of the sleeve.

Rows 1-48: Work following chart, increasing as shown. For smaller sizes, adjust pattern by working 1 (2) fewer stitches on each side of chart.

BO sep all stitches.

Make second sleeve.

Finishing

Sew the underarm seams of the sleeves by seaming the side A edges to the other side A edges, then repeat for side B. Sew the sleeves into the armholes in the same way: sides A and B separately. Weave in all ends. Sew buttons on both sides of the sweater, so that the sweater can be reversed.

Hat

The hat may be done flat (as written) or on a circular needle. The chart and directions are for a medium hat, but you can easily adjust the size by adding or subtracting a multiple of 4 stitches.

Using smaller needles and ribbing color, cast on 104 stitches.

Rows 1-13: Work in kl, p1 ribbing for 1-1/2".

Row 14: Tie on the second color and change to larger needles. Establish DSPs across the entire row as you did for the body of the sweater, keeping an OES on both edges of the hat.

Row 15: Begin following chart (start with row 15). DK to end of row as follows: work the first 4 pairs of chart, then work the 12-pair repeat eight times, then the DK the final 4 pairs. Turn.

Rows 16-63: DK to end of row as established. Turn.

Row 64: Work 1 DSP, *k2tog, p2tog, repeat from * until 1 pair remains, DK last pair.

Break off both yarns leaving long strands. Thread color A onto a sewing up needle and pull it through all color A stitches. Repeat for color B. Pull both strands tightly and weave in ends. Use color A to sew the back seam on the color A side of hat; use color B to sew the back seam on the color B side of hat. Sew a big button right on top for a nice finish.

Nordic Summer hat chart

12-pair Repeat

DOUBLE KNITTING

Twice as Nice
More for Your 4-Year Old

This child's raglan cardigan is worked in Double Knitting from the neck down. The front bands (including buttonholes) are worked simultaneously with the sweater body. At the underarms, the sleeve stitches are put on holders and the remainder of the body is worked down in one piece, ending with the lower ribbing. The sleeves are worked from the shoulder to the cuffs, leaving only small underarm seams to be stitched by hand. The neckband is picked up from the cast-on. For the hat, see Double Knit Bonnets on page 32; matching hat chart is on page 73.

Finished Size:
    Circumference: 33"
    Length from hem to underarm: 10"
    Armhole depth: 7.5"

Gauge: 18 DSPs and 24 rows = 4 in

Materials: 850 yds each of 2 colors of fingering weight yarn.

Needles: 24" circular needles and dp needles in US 4 (3.5 mm)

Notions: 2 markers, sewing needle, 10 buttons

Note: To adjust the body and/or sleeve length, add or subtract rows in the polka-dot area of the pattern.

Body

Using 24" circular needle and color A, CO 35 stitches. Loosely tie on color B and establish DK (see *Establishing DSPs* on page 10) as follows: *Byb, using color A, knit the first stitch and leave it on the left-hand needle, byf, using color B, purl

DOUBLE KNITTING

the same stitch and remove it from the left-hand needle. Repeat from * to end of row. This turns each stitch of the foundation row into a DSP.

Set-Up Row (not shown on chart): Keep an OES (see *Edge Stitches* on page 14), DK 2 pairs (for front), pm, DK 4 pairs (sleeve), pm, DK 23 pairs (back), pm, DK 4 pairs (sleeve), pm, DK 2 pairs (front). Turn.

Row 1: Begin following chart (start with row 1), working from right to left across front, then sleeve, then work the back, then sleeve, then second front (see *Reading Charts* on page 17). Work this row as follows: Keep an OES, work 1 DSP, inc 1 DSP (ncck increase), DK according to charts, increasing 1 DSP on both sides of each marker. When 1 pair remains, inc 1 DSP, work last pair. Turn. (10 pairs increased in this row.)

Rows 2-13: Continue as established, increasing as shown on chart.

Row 14: OES, work 1 DSP, inc 1 DSP, DK across row, increasing both sides of each marker as established to last pair, inc 1 DSP, work last pair. Before turning, using color A only, CO 7 stitches (not pairs) for front band (not shown on chart). Turn.

Row 15: Sl 1 p'wise, work 7 stitches in k1, p1 ribbing. Pick up color B and twist the 2 colors to prevent a hole. DK across row. After last pair, using color A only, CO 7 stitches for front band. Turn.

Note: For the rest of this pattern, FB (Front Band) means:

 - at the beginning of each row, sl 1 p'wise, work 7 stitches in k1, p1 ribbing. Pick up second color, twist colors A and B to avoid a hole where the band meets the Double Knitting, start working DK.

 - at the end of each row when 8 stitches remain, drop non-border color on the side of your work closest to you and, using border color only, work 7 stitches in k1, p1 ribbing, k1.

Rows 16-50: FB, DK across row, increasing as shown on chart, FB. Work buttonhole on row 37. Turn.

Row 51: armholes: FB, DK 33 pairs (front), place 56 pairs on holder (sleeve) and, using both colors, CO 2 pairs for underarm, DK across 73 pairs (back), place 56 pairs on holder (sleeve) and, using both colors, CO 2 pairs for underarm, DK 33 (front), FB. Turn.

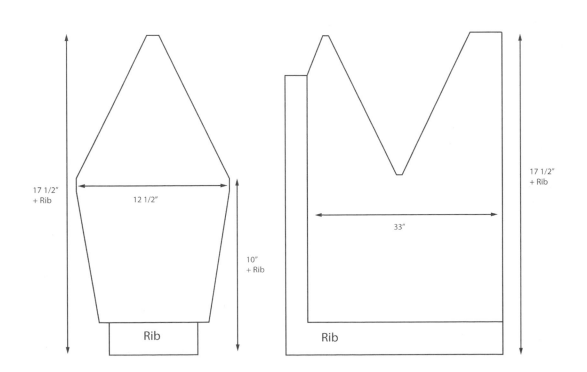

17 1/2" + Rib

12 1/2"

10" + Rib

Rib

33"

17 1/2" + Rib

Rib

Twice as Nice body chart

Pivot Stitch

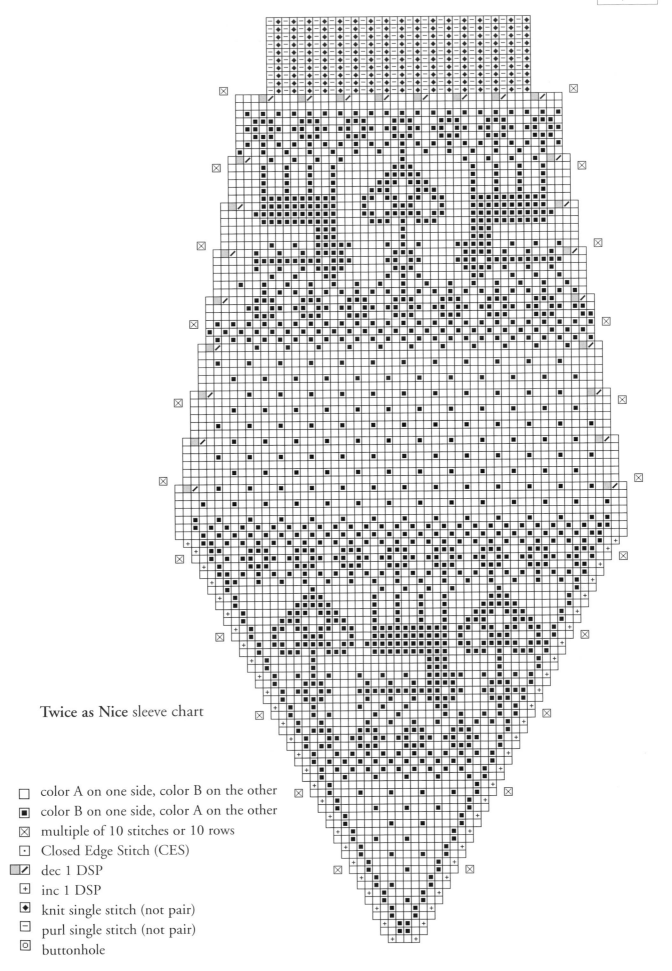

Twice as Nice sleeve chart

☐ color A on one side, color B on the other

▣ color B on one side, color A on the other

⊠ multiple of 10 stitches or 10 rows

⊡ Closed Edge Stitch (CES)

▨◪ dec 1 DSP

⊞ inc 1 DSP

◈ knit single stitch (not pair)

⊟ purl single stitch (not pair)

⊡ buttonhole

Rows 52-105: FB, DK 143 pairs following chart, FB. Turn. Work buttonholes on rows 62 and 87, as shown on chart.

Row 106: FB, tie off color B and, using color A only, work *k2tog, p2tog, repeat from * to end of DK section. You may need to start with p2tog to keep ribbing intact, FB. Turn.

Rows 107-117: Work in ribbing, making a buttonhole on row 111 as shown on chart.

BO all stitches loosely in ribbing.

Sleeves

Move the 56 sleeve stitches to dp or short circular needles. Using both colors, CO 2 pairs at the underarm and join for circular knitting. Place marker between the 2 new stitches.

Round 53-107: DK around, following chart and decreasing where shown.

Round 108: Tie off color B, using color A only, work *k2tog, p2tog, repeat from * to end of round.

Round 109: decrease: Work 2 DSPs, *dec 1 DSP, work 3 DSPs, repeat from * 7 times more (34 stitches remain).

Rounds 110-119: Work k1, p1 ribbing.

BO all stitches loosely in ribbing.

Knit second sleeve.

Neck Band

Using color A only, knit up 73 stitches around neck edge, including front bands (see *Pick Up vs Knit Up* on page 16). Work k1, p1, ribbing for 1.5", putting in a buttonhole on appropriate band after 6 rows. BO all stitches loosely in ribbing.

Finishing

With yarn threaded on a tapestry needle, sew underarm seam. Weave in loose ends. Sew buttons on both sides of button band, so that the sweater can be worn with either side out.

Matching cap: the chart is shown here and the instructions are in *Double Knit Bonnets*, page 32

□ color A on front, color B on back
■ color B on front, color A on back
⊠ multiple of 10 stitches or 10 rows
▨ dec 1 DSP
⊞ inc 1 DSP

Twice as Nice bonnet chart

Double Exposure Jacket
plus
Calico Corners Patchwork Jacket

These two jackets are almost identical in construction, but use different charts.

Double Exposure has motifs that change from light to dark along the body and sleeves, creating a subtle color change and teases the eye. The Raglan Stripes are done in Double Knit Ribbing.

The *Calico Corners Patchwork Jacket* has a fun, at-home look and can be turned to the other side for a change. The Raglan Stripes on this one are done in regular Double Knitting.

They are both seamless, neck-down raglans worked in one piece to the underarms. Put the sleeve stitches on hold and work the body to the lower edge. Pick up the sleeve stitches and work in the round to the cuffs. The ribbed front band stitches are incorporated into the body as you Double Knit.

The two-color, reversible ribbing looks the same on both sides, but is inelastic. Use three-stitch applied I-Cord to finish the front edges, and work I-Cord ties to hold the front closed. The ties can be pulled from one side to the other, depending upon which side of the jacket is worn on the outside.

Finished Size:
> Circumference: 42.5"
> Length from hem to underarm: 17"
> Armhole depth: 10.5"

Materials: 1100 yards each of two colors of fingering weight wool.

Gauge: 24 DSPs and 32 rows = 4"

Needles: 16" and 24" circular needles, straight needles, and dp needles in US 3 (3 mm), two extra circular needles in a size close to US 3 (US 2, 3, 4, or 5)

Notions: Stitch markers, crochet hook

Body

The entire body is worked back and forth from the neck down. On the odd-numbered rows, read the chart from right to left. On the even-numbered rows, read the chart from left to right (see *Reading Charts* on page 17).

Using 24" circular needle and one strand of color A, cast on 91 stitches for *Double Exposure*, or 95 stitches for *Calico Corners*.

Set-Up Row: Using color A, *k1, p1, repeat from * to end of row.

Row 1: Sl 1 p'wise, establish DK as follows: *k into front and back of next st, repeat from * to end of row (see *Establishing DSPs* on page 10). Turn.

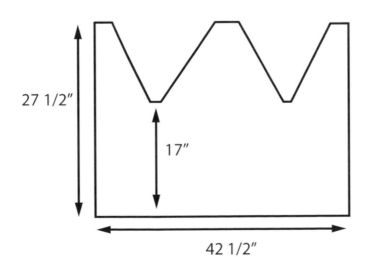
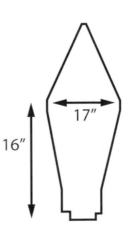

27 1/2"

17"

42 1/2"

16"

17"

Row 2: Loosely tie on color B and work *Double Knit Ribbing* (see page 15) to last pair and k the pair as one stitch using both strands. Turn.

Rows 3-9: Sl 1 single stitch p'wise, work Double Knit Ribbing as established, keeping Closed Edge Stitch (CES - see *Edge Stitches* on page 14) on both edges.

Note: For the rest of this pattern, FB (Front Band) means:
  - at the beginning of each row, sl 1 p'wise, work 7 pairs in Double Knit Ribbing, twist colors A and B to avoid a hole where the band meets the Double Knitting.
  - at the end of each row, work 7 pairs in DK Ribbing, k1.

Row 10: Work in DK Ribbing as established, but place markers to prepare for Double Knitting as follows: FB, pm, work 9 pairs (front section), pm, work 5 pairs (raglan line), pm, work 7 pairs (sleeve), pm, work 5 pairs (raglan line), pm, work 23 pairs (back), pm, work 5 pairs (raglan line), pm, work 7 pairs (sleeve), pm, work 5 pairs (raglan line), pm, work 9 pairs (front section), pm, FB. Turn.

Note: You can choose to do the raglan stripes as written here, in Double Knit Ribbing, or you can use regular Double Knitting in either stripes or a solid color. Whichever you choose, be consistent.

Row 11: This is the most intricate row, but bear with me. It includes the first raglan increases and converts some front band stitches into Double Knitting stitches. When there are two sets of numbers, the first is for *Double Exposure* and the number in parentheses is for *Calico Corners*.

With dp needle, work edge stitch and 13 pairs in DK Ribbing. Cork the ends of this needle (these stitches will be worked again later).
DK 2 (3) pairs, inc 1 DSP, DK Ribbing 5 pairs for raglan stripe, inc 1 DSP, work 5 (7) pairs for sleeve, inc 1 DSP, DK Ribbing 5 pairs for raglan stripe, inc 1 DSP, DK 21 (23) pairs for back, inc 1 DSP, DK Ribbing 5 pairs for raglan stripe, inc 1 DSP, work 5 (7) pairs for sleeve, inc 1 DSP, DK Ribbing 5 stitches for raglan stripe, inc 1 DSP,

work 2 (3) pairs for front. Place remaining 14 pairs on another dpn and cork the ends so the stitches do not fall off. Turn.

(continued on page 81)

DOUBLE KNITTING

continue on next page

DOUBLE KNITTING

☐ color A on one side, color B on the other
■ color B on one side, color A on the other
⊠ multiple of 10 stitches or 10 rows
⊡ Edge Stitch (ES)
▨ dec 1 DSP
⊞ inc 1 DSP
◆ knit stitch in DK Ribbing
⊟ purl stitch in DK Ribbing
⊡ buttonhole

Pivot Stitch

Double Exposure Jacket body chart
Knitted from the neck. Begin here and continue on page 79. Sleeve chart on page 80.

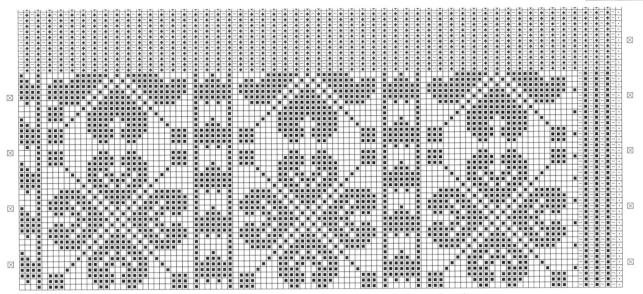

The row below is on the needles as you continue the chart.

Double Exposure
sleeve chart

Pivot Stitch

DOUBLE KNITTING

Row 12: Ignore the DSPs on the dp needle. Byb, sl 1 DSP p'wise, DK according to chart, keeping the front bands and raglan stripes in DK Ribbing. At the end of the row, uncork the dp needle and work 2 DSPs from the ribbing stitches. Re-cork the needle. Turn.

Row 13: Byb, sl 1 DSP p'wise, DK according to chart, increasing on both sides of each raglan stripe as you did on row 11. At the end of the row, uncork the dp needle and work 2 DSPs from the ribbing stitches. Re-cork the needle. Turn.

Row 14-17: Continue as established, adding stitches from the dp needles at the end of each row as shown on chart. You now have an edge stitch and 7 DSPs on each of the dp needles.

Row 18: Byb, sl 1 DSP, work according to chart. At the end of the row, uncork the dp needle and work 7 pairs in DK Ribbing for front band, CES. Turn.

Row 19: CES, work 7 pairs in DK Ribbing, DK according to chart, increasing as established. At the end of the row, uncork the dp needle and work 7 pairs in DK Ribbing for front band, CES. Turn.

Rows 20-79: Keep edges and raglan stripes as established and DK according to chart. Turn.

Row 80: armholes: Work edge as established, DK to front sleeve stitches. Remove marker, and work 3 pairs in DK Ribbing. *Place 2 pairs (ribbing) of the front raglan stripe, 75 pairs from sleeve, and 2 pairs (ribbing) of the back raglan stripe on holder 79 pairs total*, work 3 pairs in DK Ribbing, DK across back stitches, work 3 pairs in DK Ribbing. Rep from * to *, then work to the end of row as established. Turn.

Row 81: Work as established to underarm. *Using both colors A and B, CO 5 stitches, adjusting the stitches so that they are in correct color order for Double Knitting*. DK across back to second underarm, repeat from * to *. DK to end of row as established. Turn.

Rows 82-194: Continue as established following chart. Turn.

Rows 195-206: Work DK Ribbing across entire row as shown on chart. Turn.

Row 207 (not shown on chart): Tie off color B. Using color A only, work *k2tog, p2tog, repeat from * to end of row. Turn.

Row 208 (not shown on chart): *K1, p1, repeat from * to end of row.

BO all stitches loosely in ribbing.

Sleeves

Put 79 DSPs from holder onto a 16" circular needle. Attach both colors A and B. In the underarm section, pick up 5 color A stitches and 5 color B stitches and place them in correct color order on the needle. Mark the center pair of these 5 as the Center Underarm. Like the Pivot St, this pair is only worked once per round.

Round 80: Working circularly and starting at underarm, work across sleeve chart to Pivot Stitch, then work the chart back to the right side.

Note: Work the Pivot Stitch and the Center Underarm pair only once.

Rounds 81-180: DK as shown on chart, decreasing where indicated.

Row 181: Work 1 DSP, dec 1 pair, work across chart and dec 1 pair near the pivot st, work back to within 3 pairs of Center Underarm, dec 1 DSP, work Center Underarm st (49 pairs).

Rows 182-205: Work in Double Knit Ribbing.

Row 206 (not shown on chart): Tie off color B. Using color A only, work *k2tog, p2tog, repeat from * to end of row. Turn.

Row 207 (not shown on chart): *K1, p1, repeat from * to end of row.

BO all stitches loosely in ribbing.

Calico Corners Patchwork Jacket
Charts are on pages 84 and 85.
To knit this jacket, use the row-by-row instructions for **Double Exposure Jacket**,
ignoring references to Pivot Stitches.

Finishing

Using color A, apply a 3-stitch I-Cord along both front openings (see *EZ's Applied I-Cord* on page 15). Weave in ends. Block lightly.

I-Cord Ties

Make six 6-stitch I-Cord tubes, as follows:

With smaller-size double-pointed needles, Cast On 6 stitches. *Slide stitches to other end of needle and firmly knit the 6 stitches.

Repeat from * until Cord is 12" long. Tie an overhand knot in one end of each cord. With a tapestry needle, neatly stitch the end down as shown on the opposite page.

Thread the yarn tail at the other end of the cord through a tapestry needle and pull it through the sweater where desired at the boundary between the fronts and front bands (see above).

Tie remaining end in overhand knot and - as shown - secure the short end to the cord.

DOUBLE KNITTING

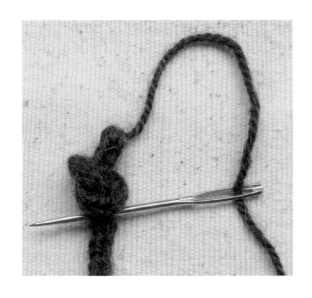

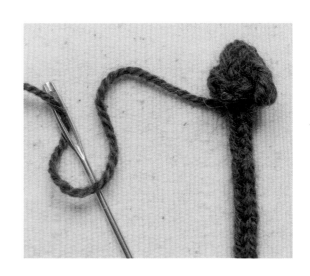

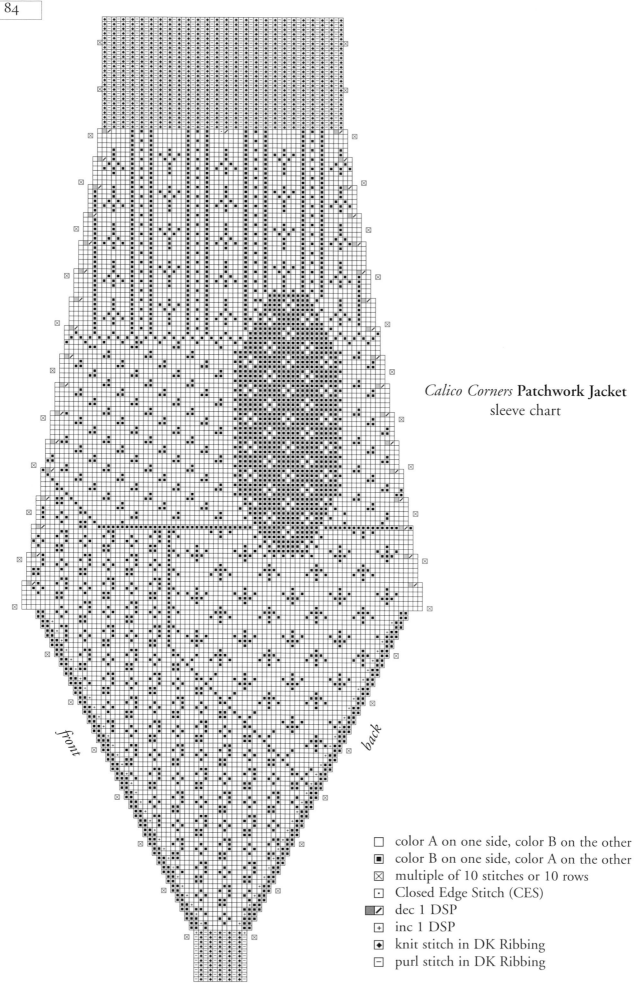

Calico Corners **Patchwork Jacket**
sleeve chart

DOUBLE KNITTING

front

back

☐	color A on one side, color B on the other
▣	color B on one side, color A on the other
⊠	multiple of 10 stitches or 10 rows
⊡	Closed Edge Stitch (CES)
◨	dec 1 DSP
+	inc 1 DSP
◈	knit stitch in DK Ribbing
⊟	purl stitch in DK Ribbing

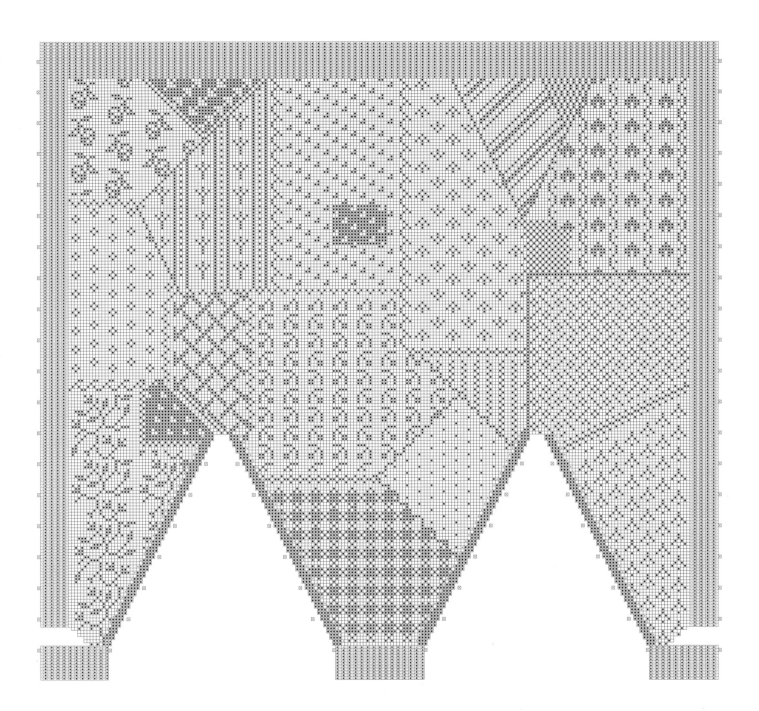

Calico Corners Patchwork Jacket body chart
Breaking this multi-faceted chart into quarters makes it difficult to follow,
so you have permission to enlarge this page for your personal use.
The sleeve chart, opposite, is a more legible size.

The Far East
A Shaped and Flowered Jacket

This V-neck, double-breasted jacket has an elegant look when worn over a contrasting turtleneck top and is a pleasure to wear both day or night.

Finished Size:
> Circumference: 64", allowing for overlap
> Length from hem to underarm: 24"
> Armhole depth: 11"

Gauge: 16 DSPs and 20 rows = 4"

Materials: 1600 yds each of 2 colors of sport weight yarn.

Needles: 16" and 29" circular needles, straight needles, and dp needles in US 5 (3.75 mm), an extra circular needle in a size close to US 4 (US 3, 4, 5, or 6)

Notions: 2 markers, sewing needle or crochet hook, 2 buttons

Body

Using 29" circular needle and two strands of color A held together, cast on 262 stitches. Turn.

Set-up Row: Loosely tie on color B and cut off one of the color A strands. Closed Edge Stitch (CES - see *Edge Stitches* on page 14), *byb, k1 with color B, byf, p1 with color A. Repeat from * until 1 single stitch remains, using color A only, knit the last stitch. You have 1 edge stitch, 261 DSPs, and 1 edge stitch. Turn.

Note: For the rest of this pattern, CES (Closed Edge Stitch) means:
 - at the beginning of each row, using color A only, sl 1 single stitch p'wise, pick up color B, twist yarns to prevent hole, continue.
 - at the end of each row, drop color B on the side of your work that is closest to you, use color A to knit last single stitch.

Row 1: Begin following chart (start with row 1): CES, DK following the chart from right to left to the Pivot Stitch, then read the same line of chart from left to right. Work the Pivot Stitch only once (see *Reading Charts* on page 17).

Rows 2-112: CES, DK following chart as established, CES.

Row 113, neck shaping: CES, DK following chart until 16 DSPs and one edge stitch remain, slip those stitches onto a holder so that the open end of the holder is toward the garment; you will add stitches to the holder in subsequent rows. Turn.

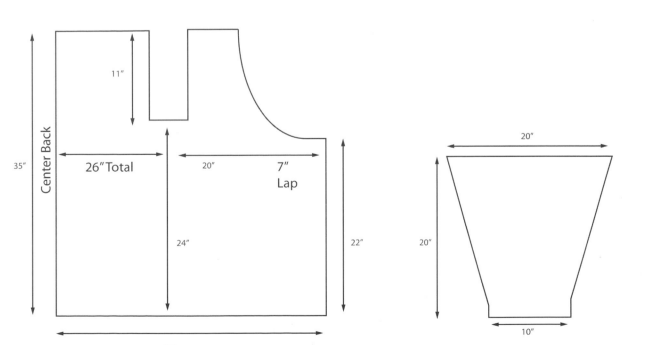

DOUBLE KNITTING

Pivot Stitch

Far East body chart

Far East sleeve chart

Chart Note: One of the 12-stitch front sections of the jacket is one row lower than the other. Work the single row shown beneath Chart C if you crave symmetry.

☐ color A on one side, color B on the other
■ color B on one side, color A on the other
☒ multiple of 10 stitches or 10 rows
⊡ Closed Edge Stitch (CES)
▨ dec 1 DSP
⊞ inc 1 DSP

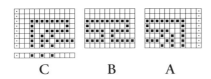

C   B   A

Far East collar charts

Row 114: Open Edge Stitch (OES - see *Edge Stitches* on page 14), DK following chart until 16 DSPs and one edge stitch remain, slip those stitches onto a second holder. Turn.

Row 115: OES, DK following chart until 5 DSPs remain, add those pairs to holder. Turn.

Row 116-124: Follow chart as established, adding stitches to holders as shown on chart.

First Front

Row 125: armholes: Work 37 DSPs. Turn.

Row 126: Keeping an OES at both edges of your work, DK following chart until 1 DSP remains; add that pair to holder. Turn.

Row 127-180: DK to armhole edge. Turn.

BO sep 23 pairs.

Second Front

Starting at the front edge of jacket, ignore the 16 pairs on hold and loosely tie on both colors. Begin at row 125 and work exactly as you did for the First Front.

Back

Put 18 DSPs from each end of the back section on holders for the underarms. Loosely tie on both colors.

Row 125: Keeping an OES at both edges of your work, DK following chart, remembering to work the Pivot Stitch only once. Turn.

Rows 126-179: Continue following chart as established.

Row 180, first shoulder: DK 23 pairs. Turn.

BO sep for first shoulder.

Row 180, center back: Put 39 pairs on hold for back of neck.

Row 180, second shoulder: Reattach colors A and B. Work 23 pairs for second shoulder. Turn.

BO sep for second shoulder.

Shoulder Seams

*Take the stitches for the front right shoulder and split them onto two needles as follows: color A stitches on one needle, color B stitches on the second needle. Repeat this process for the right shoulder stitches from the back of the coat. Using color A, weave or sew together the color A shoulders. Turn to the other side and weave or sew the color B stitches. Repeat from * for left shoulder stitches.

Sleeves

The sleeves are worked from the top of the sleeve to the bottom. Work back and forth for 18 rows, then join and knit circularly. All the sleeve decreases are made at the underarm and I like to leave one stitch on either side of the marking ring and then decrease.

Set-Up Round: Loosely tie on color A at one edge of the armhole. Using a spare circular needle (similar in size to your working size), and with side A facing, Knit Up 81 stitches (see *Pick Up vs Knit Up* on page 16) around the sleeve opening, but do not include the 18 DSPs that are on hold. Turn to the color B side of the garment and, using another spare needle, Knit Up 81 stitches around side B.

Row 1, begin chart: Using a 16" circular needle, begin Double Knitting as follows: Hold the side A stitches and side B stitches parallel. *Byb, using color A, k1 from side A needle, byf, using color B, p1 from side B needle. Repeat from * until all but 1 DSP are on righthand needle. For the last pair, dec 1 DSP, which will use the last pair from the sleeve and the first pair of the 18 on hold. Turn.

Rows 2-18: DK following chart to last pair, dec 1 DSP as in row 1. Turn.

Round 19-100: DK following chart decreasing where indicated.

Round 101 (not shown on chart): Drop color B and, using color A only, *k1, p1, repeat from * around.

Bind off as follows: K2tog, *p2tog, pass stitch over, k2tog, pass stitch over, repeat from * to end of round.

Make second sleeve.

Collar

Use a circular needle to prepare for the collar as follows: Move the 48 pairs from one of the front holders onto the needle, pick up 19 pairs along the straight edge of the collar, move the 39 stitches from back neck holder onto needle, pick up 18 pairs along other side of neck, move 48 pairs from second front. You now have 172 pairs.

Row 1: Begin following chart as follows: CES, work 10 stitches from Collar Chart A, repeat Collar Chart B 15 times, work 11 stitches from Collar Chart C, CES. Turn. You now have 171 pairs and 2 edge stitches.

Rows 2-8: CES, DK to within 1 stitch of end of row, CES.

Row 9 (not shown on chart): Drop color B and, using color A only, *k1, p1, repeat from * around.

Bind off as follows: K2tog, *p2tog, pass stitch over, k2tog, pass stitch over, repeat from * to end of row.

Finishing

Work a buttonhole loop at the top corner on each front with a needle or crochet hook. Sew buttons on each side so you can overlap and button with either side worn out.

Sonja Henie
A Norwegian Yoke Jacket

Soft, snugly and simple to make is this jacket with a yoke that fits all shoulders. Work the body and sleeves to the underarm, then unite all stitches onto one needle to work the yoke. It is made with two soft grays and it looks like snow laden clouds and would be warm enough for any ski weekend.

Finished Size:
> Circumference: 50 in, allowing for overlap
> Length from hem to underarm: 16 in
> Overall Length: 25 in

Gauge: 20 DSPs and 28 rows = 4"

Materials: 1000 yds each of 2 colors of sport weight yarn.

Needles: 24" circular needles in size US 1 (1.5 mm) and US 3 (3.0 mm)

Notions: Markers, sewing needle, 18 buttons

Body

Using color A and smaller needle, CO 251 stitches. The first and last 9 stitches are the front bands, so you may want to mark them.

Rows 1-7: Work in k1, p1 ribbing, slipping the first stitch p'wise on each row.

Row 8, buttonhole: Work in k1, p1 ribbing, inserting a buttonhole of your choice in the center of the 9-stitch front band on one side.

Rows 9-22: Work in k1, p1 ribbing, slipping the first stitch p'wise on each row.

Row 23: Establish Double Knitting as follows (see *Establishing DSPs* on page 10) as follows: slip the first st, work 8 stitches in ribbing as established, pm. Still using only color A, k and p in each stitch across to the last 9 stitches, pm, rib 9 stitches for front band. You now have 9 single stitches for the front band, 233 DSPs, and 9 single stitches for other front band.

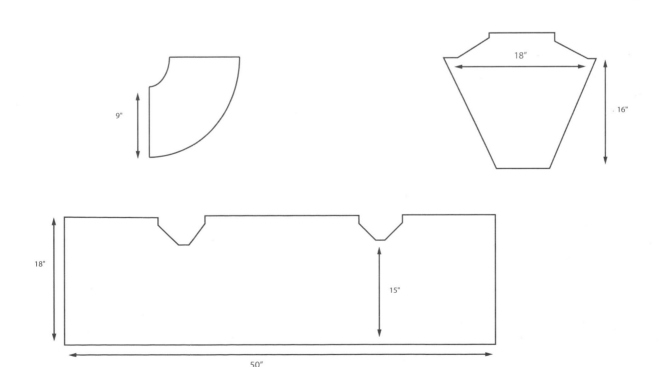

Pivot Stitch

Sonja Henie lower body chart

Note: For the rest of this pattern, **FB** (Front Band) means:
- at the beginning of each row, sl 1 single stitch p'wise, work 8 stitches in k1, p1 ribbing.
- at the end of each row, using color A only, work 7 stitches in k1, p1 ribbing, k1.

Row 24: Change to larger needle and begin following chart (start on row 24). Work from right to left until the Pivot Stitch, then work across the same row from left to right (only knit Pivot Stitch once) as follows: FB, loosely tie on color B, *byb, k1 with color B, byf, p1 with color A, repeat from * to next marker, FB.

Rows 25-110: FB, DK to next marker, FB. Turn. Work buttonholes on rows 31, 54, 77, and 100 as indicated on chart.

Row 111, underarms: FB, work 52 DSPs, BO sep 14 DSPs, work 100 DSPs, BO sep 14 DSPs, work 51 DSPs, FB. The final two stitches from each of the bound-off sections are added to the count, so you now have 52 DSPs (plus front bands) for each front section and 101 DSPs for the back. Stop and make sleeves.

DOUBLE KNITTING

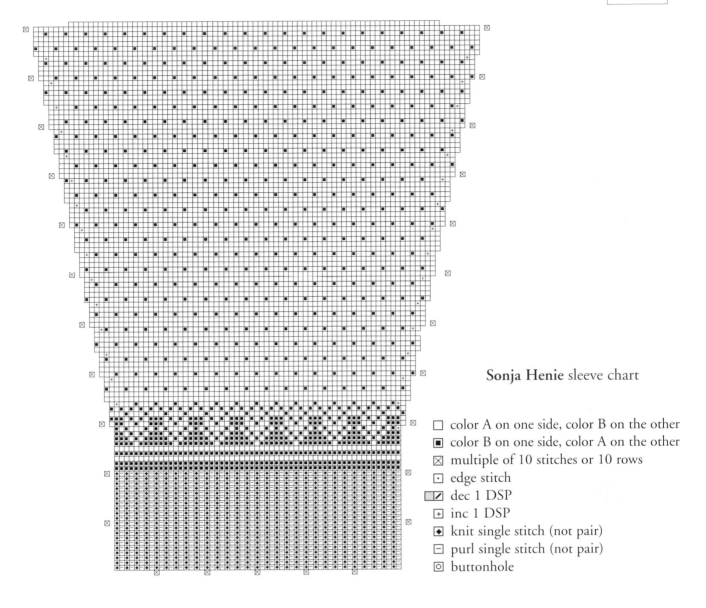

Sonja Henie sleeve chart

☐ color A on one side, color B on the other
■ color B on one side, color A on the other
⊠ multiple of 10 stitches or 10 rows
· edge stitch
▨ dec 1 DSP
⊞ inc 1 DSP
◆ knit single stitch (not pair)
⊟ purl single stitch (not pair)
⊡ buttonhole

Sleeves

Make two sleeves, working in the round so there are no seams. Using color A and smaller needle, CO 58 stitches. Join for circular knitting and pm.

Rounds 1-20: Work in k1, p1 ribbing for 20 rows.

Round 21: Establish DK as follows: Using color B, k and p in each stitch around, pm. You now have 58 DSPs.

Round 22: Change to larger needle and begin following chart (start with row 22). DK entire round.

Rounds 23-110: Continue as established, increasing where indicated.

Round 111: BO sep 8 DSPs, DK until 7 DSPs remain, BO sep 7 DSPs. 75 DSPs remain.

Yoke

Row 1: Follow row 1 of Yoke Chart: FB, DK 52 pairs for front, pm, DK 75 pairs from first sleeve, pm, DK 101 pairs from back, pm, DK 75 pairs from second sleeve, pm, DK 52 pairs for front, FB. Turn.

Row 2: FB, *DK to within 3 pairs of marker, dec 1 DSP, work 2 DSPs, dec 1 DSP, repeat from * three times more, then DK to final marker, FB.

Sonja Henie *yoke chart*

Pivot Stitch

Rows 3-21: Work as established, decreasing where indicated.

Row 22 decrease: FB, DK 4 pairs, *dec 1 DSP, work 7 DSPs, repeat from * until 4 DSPs remain, work them, FB (34 pairs decreased).

Rows 23-37: Follow the chart, keeping front bands in ribbing as established. The chart is 17 stitches narrower to account for the 34 pairs you just decreased; the motifs won't line up as shown. The Pivot Stitch is always the far left stitch on the chart. See the photo of the sweater for a more accurate portrayal of the alignment of the motifs.

Note: Work a buttonhole on row 35.

Row 38 decrease: FB, DK 2 pairs, *dec 1 DSP, work 7 DSPs, repeat from * until 4 DSPs remain, work them, FB (36 pairs decreased).

Rows 39-43: Work as established.

Row 44 decrease: FB, DK 2 pairs, *dec 1 DSP, work 6 pairs, repeat from * sixteen times more, dec 1 DSP, work 5 pairs, ** dec 1 DSP, work 6 pairs, repeat from ** until 2 pairs remain, work them, FB (36 pairs decreased).

Rows 45-78: Work as established, including decreases and buttonholes as shown on chart.

Row 79 decrease: Change to smaller needle: FB, *k2tog, p2tog, repeat from * until end of DK, FB.

Rows 80-87: Work in k1, p1 ribbing. **Note:** Work a buttonhole on row 81.

BO all stitches.

Finishing: Sew or weave underarms separately (weave side A to side A, and B to B). Sew buttons on both side of one band. Wait for snow.

DOUBLE KNITTING

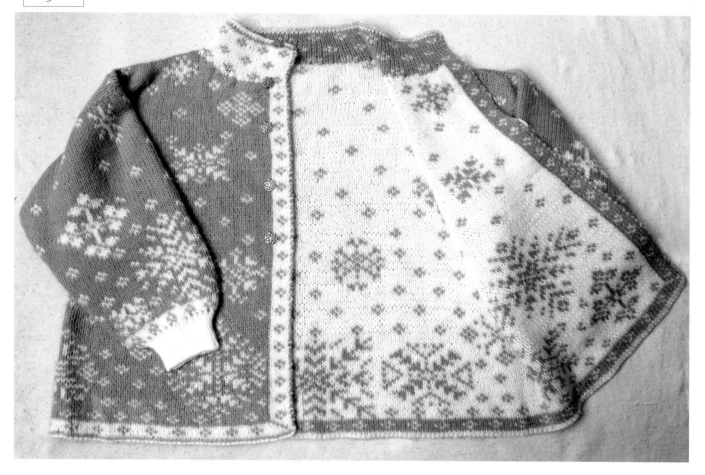

The North Star

I grew up in Seattle, where I learned to ski at Snoqualmie Pass Ski Areap; riding the special ski train that had been arranged for area schools. After I moved to Idaho and skied at Sun Valley, I was convinced that every Scandinavian and German who came to America became a ski instructor.

This is a semi-cropped jacket with a high collar and a ribbed, cuffed sleeve. It is worked from the bottom hem to the armholes and then divided into sections and knit to the shoulder. The sleeves are cast on around the armhole and worked down to the cuff. For buttonholes, I crocheted an edging up the front and made buttonholes as I went, but an I-Cord edge with I-Cord buttonholes will work just as well. The cowl is optional, and is knit in the round without a seam.

Finished Size:
   Circumference: 44"
   Length from hem to underarm: 12"

Overall Length: 20"

Gauge: 20 DSPs and 20 rows = 4 in

Materials: 1600 yds each of 2 colors of sport weight yarn for coat, 600 yds of each color for the cowl.

Needles: 16" and 29" circular needles and straight needles in size US 7 (4.5 mm), double-point needles in US 5 (3.75 mm), an extra circular needle in a size close to US 7 (US 5, 6, 7, or 8)

Notions: Markers, sewing needle, 10 buttons

Jacket

Using 29" circular needle and two strands of color A held together, cast on 218 stitches. Turn.

Set-up Row: Loosely tie on color B and cut off one of the color A strands. Closed Edge Stitch (CES - see *Edge Stitches* on page 14), *byb, k1 with color B, byf, p1 with color A. Repeat from * until 1 single stitch remains, using color A only, knit the last stitch. You have 1 edge stitch, 217 DSPs, and 1 edge stitch. Turn.

Note: For the rest of this pattern, CES (Closed Edge Stitch) means:

- at the beginning of each row, using color A only, sl 1 single stitch p'wise, pick up color B, twist yarns to prevent hole, continue.

- at the end of each row, drop color B on the side of your work that is closest to you, use color A to knit last single stitch.

Row 1: Begin following chart (begin with row 1) work as follows: CES, DK until a single stitch remains, CES. Turn.

Rows 2-86: CES, DK to final edge stitch, CES. Turn.

Row 87: underarms: CES, DK 56 pairs, BO sep 3 pairs, DK 98 pairs, BO sep 3 pairs, DK 55 pairs, CES. Turn. **Note:** The final two stitches from each of the bound-off sections are added to the count, so you now have 56 DSPs for each front section and 99 DSPs for the back. Turn.

First Front

Row 88: Using another needle, CES, DK to first armhole. Keep an Open Edge Stitch (OES) at the armhole edge (make sure that the two colors are **not** twisted at the armhole edge). Leave the back and the other front on the circular needle, corking the ends and continue on the first front. Turn.

Rows 89-127: DK following chart, keeping a CES at the border edge and an OES at the armhole edge.

Row 128: neck shaping: CES, DK 13 pairs. Slip those onto a holder so that the open end of the holder is toward the garment; you will add stitches to the holder in subsequent rows. DK to end of row. Turn.

Row 129: DK entire row. Turn.

Row 130: DK 4 pairs and add them to the holder, DK to end of row. Turn.

Row 131: DK entire row. Turn.

Row 132: DK 3 pairs and add them to the holder, DK to end of row. Turn.

Row 133: DK entire row. Turn.

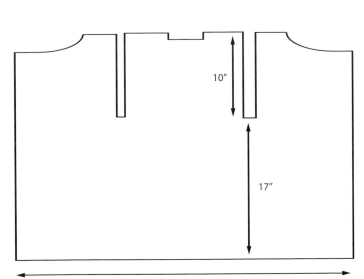

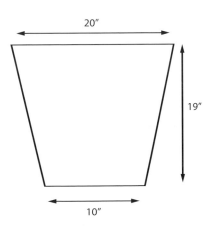

North Star body chart

DOUBLE KNITTING

☐ color A on one side, color B on the other
■ color B on one side, color A on the other
☒ multiple of 10 stitches or 10 rows
▨ dec 1 DSP

North Star sleeve chart

DOUBLE KNITTING

Row 134: DK 3 pairs and add them to the holder, DK to end of row. Turn.

Row 135: DK entire row. Turn.

Row 136: DK 2 pairs and add them to the holder, DK to end of row. Turn.

Row 137: BO 9 DSPs, DK to end of row. Turn.

Row 138: DK 2 pairs and add them to the holder, DK to end of row. Turn.

Row 139: BO sep 10 DSPs, DK to end of row. Turn.

BO sep 10 pairs.

Second Front

Starting at the front edge of jacket, loosely tie on both colors. Begin at row 88 and work exactly as you did for the First Front, following appropriate chart.

Back

Row 88: Loosely tie on both yarns. Keep an OES on both armhole edges and DK entire row. Turn.

Row 89-136: DK entire row according to chart. Turn.

Row 137, shoulder shaping: BO sep 9 DSPs, DK to end of row. Turn.

Row 138: BO sep 9 DSPs, DK to end of row. Turn.

Row 139: BO sep 10 pairs, DK 10 pairs. Turn.

BO sep 10 pairs.

Row 139, second shoulder: Move 41 pairs to a holder at the center back. Loosely tie on both colors at the neck edge and DK to end of row. Turn.

Row 140: BO sep 10 pairs, DK to end of row. Turn.

BO sep 10 pairs.

Shoulder Seams

*Take the stitches for front right shoulder and split them onto two needles as follows: color A stitches on one needle, color B stitches on the second needle. Repeat this process for right shoulder stitches from the back of the coat. Using color A, weave or sew together the color A shoulders. Turn to the other side and weave or sew the color B stitches. Repeat from * for left shoulder stitches.

Sleeves

The sleeves are worked from the shoulder down to the ribbed cuff. I decreased and narrowed them as I went, just a little. I knit them on circular needles so there is no seam anywhere. I put the entire jacket together before working the sleeves because I needed to try it on and see how long the sleeves needed to be. I decided to have bloused sleeves with a ribbed cuff so that it would fit a variety of sizes. Alter the sleeve length as you like.

Set-Up Round: Loosely tie on color A at one edge of the armhole. Using a spare circular needle (similar in size to your working size), and with side A facing, Knit Up 103 stitches around the sleeve opening (see *Pick Up vs Knit Up* on page 16). Turn to the color B side of the garment and, using another spare needle, Knit Up 103 stitches around side B.

Round 1, begin chart: Using a 16" circular needle, begin Double Knitting as follows: Hold the side A stitches and side B stitches parallel. *Byb, using color A, k1 from side A needle, byf, using color B, p1 from side B needle. Repeat from * until all DSPs are on right-hand needle. Pm for center underarm.

Round 2: DK all pairs following chart.

Round 3, decrease round: DK 1 pair, dec 1 DSP, DK around until 3 pairs remain, dec 1 DSP, work 1 pair.

Rounds 4-82: DK all pairs, decreasing as shown on chart.

Round 83: Work as established, but this round has an extra decrease (shown on chart) so you have an even number of stitches for the ribbing.

Round 84: Tie off one color. *K2tog, p2tog, repeat from * for entire round.

Rounds 85-96: Work in k1, p1 ribbing. Bind off all stitches.

Collar

The collar is about 5" - 6" deep and is a continuation of the front band. The collar is worked in Double Knitting.

Picking up: Tie on both yarns at one of the front edges. Use the appropriate color for the front band (it depends on where you begin) and a larger size 16" circular needle.

Set-Up Row: You want to knit up stitches and make increases so that there are no gaps between the body and the collar.

It is important to have a smooth transition, so don't worry as much about the numbers. Here is what I did: CES, DK 13 pairs, inc 1 DSP, DK 4 pairs, inc 1 DSP, *DK 3 pairs, inc 1 DSP*, repeat

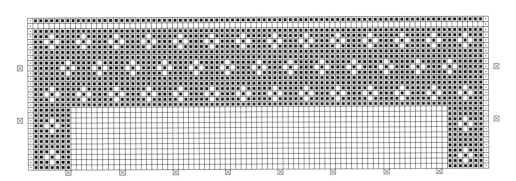

North Star collar chart

from * to * one more time, **DK 2 pairs, inc 1 DSP**, repeat from ** to ** one more time.

You are now to the shoulder. DK across 41 stitches on hold at back of neck. Repeat the pick ups for second side reversing the numbers. You now have 107 pairs on your needle and an edge stitch on each edge. Turn.

Row 1: In this row, you must decrease the number of stitches to 86, but work the edge stitches and first/last seven stitches in cross pattern (see row 1 on chart) as follows: CES, work 7 DSPs according to the chart, dec as needed across the center section so that you have 7 DSPs and one edge stitch remaining, work them as established.

Rows 2-29: CES, DK until 1 single stitch remains, CES.

Bind off as follows: K2tog, *p2tog, pass stitch over, k2tog, pass stitch over, repeat from * to end of row.

Finishing

Work buttonhole loops (crochet or I-Cord) along the front edge. Sew buttons on each side so you can button with either side worn out. Weave in any loose ends, and you're finished.

North Star cowl

Cowl

Using color A and larger needles, cast on 230 stitches. Join into a circle.

Round 1: Loosely tie on color B and, working in the round, *byb, k1 in color B, byf, p1 in color A, repeat from *. You have 115 DSPs.

Rounds 2-112: DK following chart.

Round 113: Tie off color B, using color A only, k230.

Bind off as follows: K1, *k1, pass first stitch over, k1, pass first stitch over, k2tog, pass first stitch over, repeat from * to end of row.

North Star cowl chart

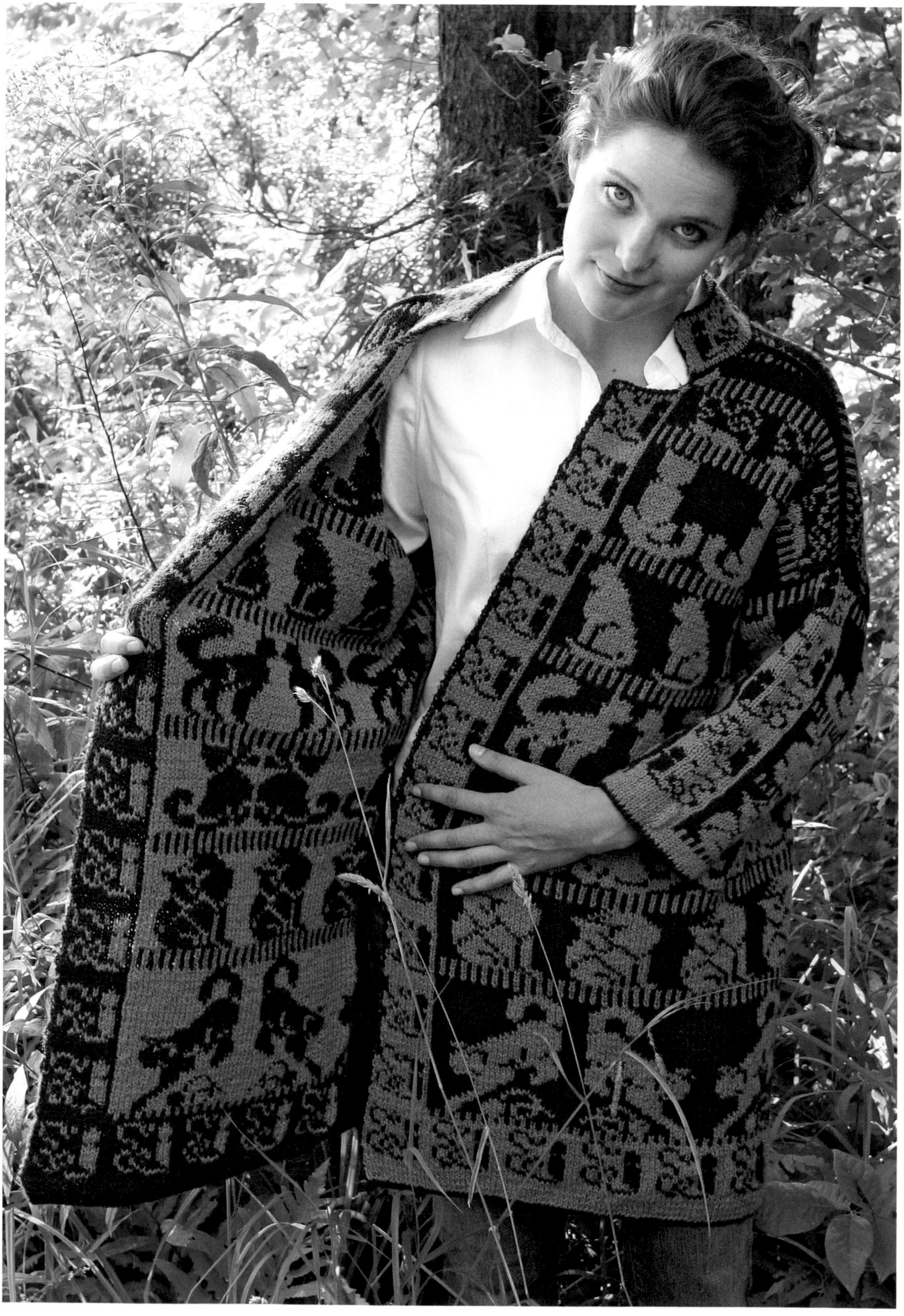

Cat and Mouse Car Coat

This comfortable car coat was designed specifically to use Shetland Jumper Weight wool in reversible Double Knitting; see the colorful Shetland version on pages 108-109.

It could also be knit in any sport weight yarn in single knitting, although some places the yarn would have to be carried quite far. That, of course, is the advantage of Double Knitting; the yarn is not stranded. I have always wanted to use a rainbow palette and am pleased with the result. If you choose, you could knit the entire design using only 2 colors, such as the one shown here - knitted by Jane Hill in Finnish *Satakieli* wool.

Finished Size:
Circumference: 46"
Length from hem to underarm: 19"
Armhole depth: 9"

Gauge: 24 DSPs and 32 rows = 4"

Materials: 2000 yds each of 2 colors of DK weight yarn for version shown opposite.

For model on pages 108-109, Jamieson & Smith 2-Ply Jumper Weight Wool: #1A natural, (11 balls), 2 balls each of the following : #FC47 medium blue; #21 dk blue; #FC56 purple blue; #133 medium purple; #FC55 red-purple; #55 dark red; #93 bright red; #125 rust; #73 orange; #91 yellow; #28 gold; #FC11 yellow green; #118 green; #FC41 dark aqua; #142 medium aqua.

Needles: 16" and 29" circular needles, straight needles, and dp needles - US 6 (4 mm), an extra circular needle in a size close to US 6 (US 4, 5, 6, or 7)

Notions: Stitch markers, 1 silk-covered snap

Body

Using 29" circular needle and two strands of color A held together, cast on 282 stitches. Turn.

Set-up Row: Loosely tie on color B and cut off one of the color A strands. Sl 1 single stitch p'wise. *Byb, k1 with color B, byf, p1 with color A. Repeat from * until 1 single stitch remains. Using color A only, knit last single stitch. You have 1 edge stitch, 281 DSPs, and 1 edge stitch. This establishes Closed Edge Stitches (CESs, see *Edge Stitches* on page 14).

Note: For the rest of this pattern, CES (Closed Edge Stitch) means:
 - at the beginning of each row, sl 1 single stitch p'wise, pick up color B and twist yarns to prevent hole, continue.
 - at the end of each row, drop color B on the side of your work closest to you and, using color A only, knit the last single stitch.

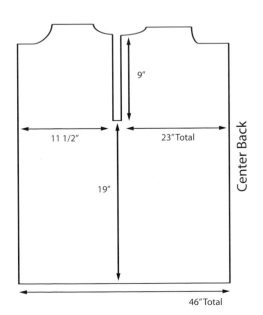

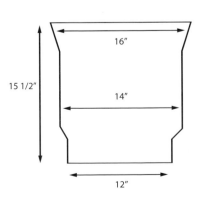

Row 1: Begin following chart (begin with row 1) as follows: CES, DK following chart to Pivot Stitch, work same row of chart from left to right repeating pattern to beginning, CES. Note: work Pivot Stitch only once, as described in *Reading Charts* on page 17. Turn.

Hint: I use lots of markers when knitting a coat such as this (instead of over-taxing my brain). On this pattern I placed markers between the bands of mice and the body. I also used markers around the cats, to facilitate counting the individual blocks of patterns. Those markers move with each series of cats.

Rows 2-152: Continue as established, following chart. If you are making the colorful version, change color B every two rows in the sequence listed in the Materials section.

Row 153, armholes: CES, DK 68 pairs, BO sep 4 DSPs (see *Binding Off* on page 13), DK 137 pairs, BO sep 4 DSPs, work 68 DSPs, CES. Turn.

First Front

Row 154: Using another needle, CES, DK to the first armhole. At the armhole edge, make an Open Edge Stitch (OES - see *Edge Stitches* on page 14). This makes picking up sleeve stitches neater. Leave the remaining stitches on the circular needle and continue with the new needle on the first front only.

Row 155-222: Continue as established following chart, keeping CES at front edge and OES at armhole edge.

Row 223, neck shaping: BO edge stitch, BO tog 13 DSPs. DK across the row. Turn.

Row 224: DK to end of row. Turn.

Row 225: Work 2 DSPs, dec 1 DSP, DK to end of row. Turn.

Row 226: shoulder shaping: BO sep 7 DSPs, DK to end of row. Turn.

Row 227-237: Continue as established following chart, decreasing where indicated.

BO sep 7 DSPs.

Center Back

Row 153: Starting at the armhole next to the front you just finished, tie on both yarns. Keep OESs at both edges of the back. Using another needle, DK to other armhole following chart. Leave the remaining stitches (second front) on circular needle and cont with new needle on center back only. Turn.

Rows 154-224: DK according to chart.

Row 225, shoulder shaping & back of neck: BO sep 7 DSPs. DK to end of row. Turn.

Row 226: BO sep 7 DSPs. DK 46 pairs. Turn.

Row 227, first shoulder: Work 1 DSP, dec 1 DSP, DK to end of row. Turn.

Row 228: BO sep 7 DSPs, work to end of row. Turn.

Row 229-237: Continue as established, binding off where shown on chart. Turn.

BO sep 7 DSPs.

Second Shoulder

Row 226: Starting at the neck edge of the back, tie on both yarns. BO sep 27 DSPs. Work 1 DSP, dec 1 pair, DK to end of row. Turn.

Row 227: BO sep 7 DSPs, work to end of row. Turn.

Row 228: Work 1 DSPs, decrease 1 pair, DK to end of row. Turn.

Rows 229-236: Continue as established, binding off where shown on chart. Turn.

BO sep 7 pairs.

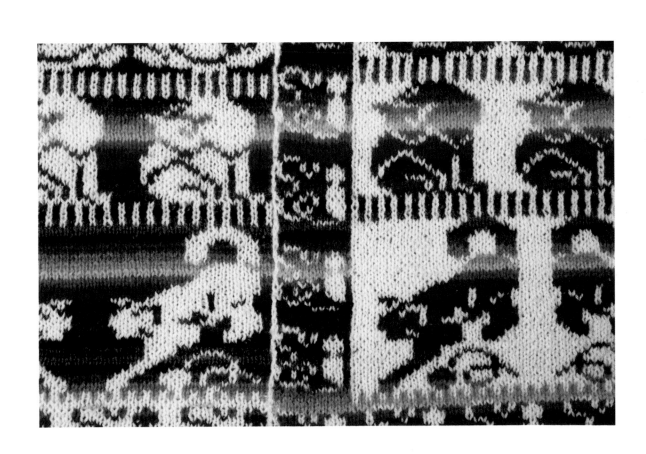

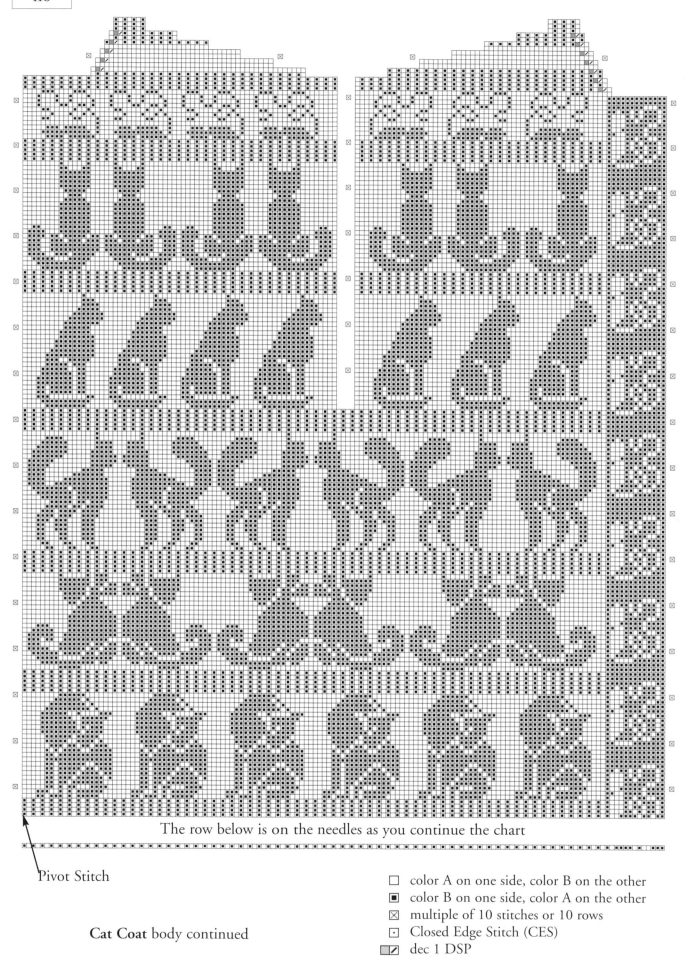

The row below is on the needles as you continue the chart

Pivot Stitch

Cat Coat body continued

☐ color A on one side, color B on the other
■ color B on one side, color A on the other
⊠ multiple of 10 stitches or 10 rows
· Closed Edge Stitch (CES)
▨ dec 1 DSP

DOUBLE KNITTING

continue on opposite page

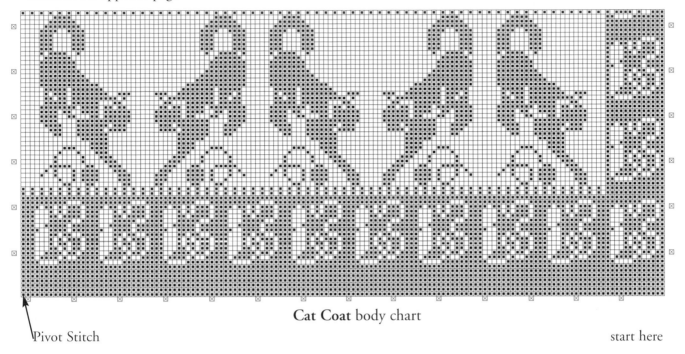

Cat Coat body chart

Pivot Stitch

start here

Second Front

Row 153: Starting at the front edge of the coat, tie on both yarns. CES, DK to armhole. At the armhole edge, keep an OES. Turn.

Rows 154-238: Work exactly as you did for First Front.

Shoulder Seams

*Take the stitches for the front right shoulder and split them onto two needles as follows: color A stitches on one needle, color B stitches on the second needle. Repeat this process for the right shoulder stitches from back of coat. Using color A, either kitchener the color A shoulder stitches together, or use 3-needle BO to unite them. Turn to the other side and BO the color B stitches. Repeat from * for left shoulder stitches.

Sleeves

The sleeves are worked in the round from the top of the sleeve to the bottom. All the sleeve decreases are made at the underarm and I like to leave one stitch on either side of the marking ring and then decrease.

Set-Up Round: On side A, starting at the center underarm, tie on color A. Using a spare circular needle, knit up 99 stitches around armhole. Leave this dangling. Turn the garment over and, at the same center underarm, tie on color B. Using another spare circular needle, knit up 99 stitches around side B.

Round 1: Using larger needle, DK around sleeve as follows: Byb, k1 from front needle, byf, p1 from back needle. After you DK 99 pairs, all stitches are on the circular needle. Pm.

Note: If you are doing the Rainbow Version, you now work the colors from the bottom of the list to the top.

Round 2: Begin following chart (start with row 2) working in the round.

Rounds 3-124: DK around sleeve following chart, decreasing where indicated.

Round 125: Loosely tie off color B and, using color A only, *k1, p1, repeat from * to end of round.

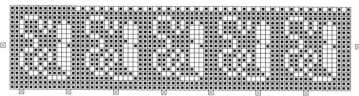

Cat Coat
collar chart

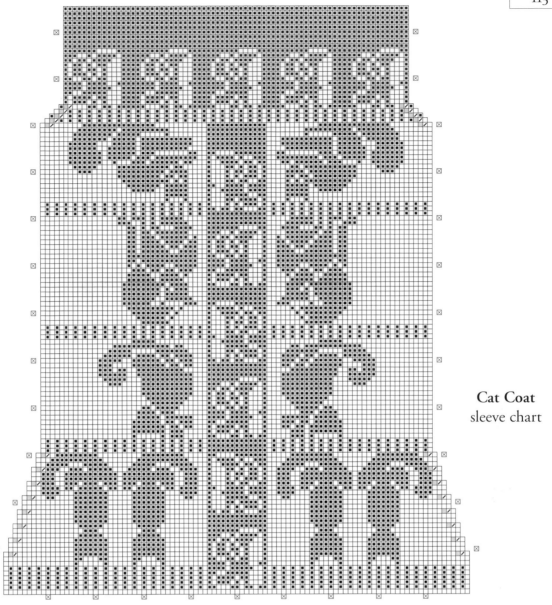

Cat Coat
sleeve chart

Round 126: K2tog, *k2tog, pass first stitch over, repeat from * to end of round to bind off all stitches. Knit second sleeve.

Collar

(chart on opposite page)

On side A, starting at front edge, tie on color A. Using a circular needle, knit up 77 stitches around neck. Leave this dangling. Turn the garment over and, at the same front edge, tie on color B. Using another circular needle, knit up 77 stitches around side B.

Set-Up Row: DK around collar as follows: Byb,

k1 from front needle, byf, p1 from back needle. After you work 77 DSPs, all stitches are on the circular needle. Turn.

Rows 1-17: DK according to chart.

Row 18: Loosely tie off color B and, using color A only, *k1, p1, repeat from * to end of row.

Row 19: K2tog, *k2tog, pass first stitch over, repeat from * to end of row to bind off all stitches.

Finishing

None. Match one of the colors to a nice pair of slacks or shirt and wear proudly.

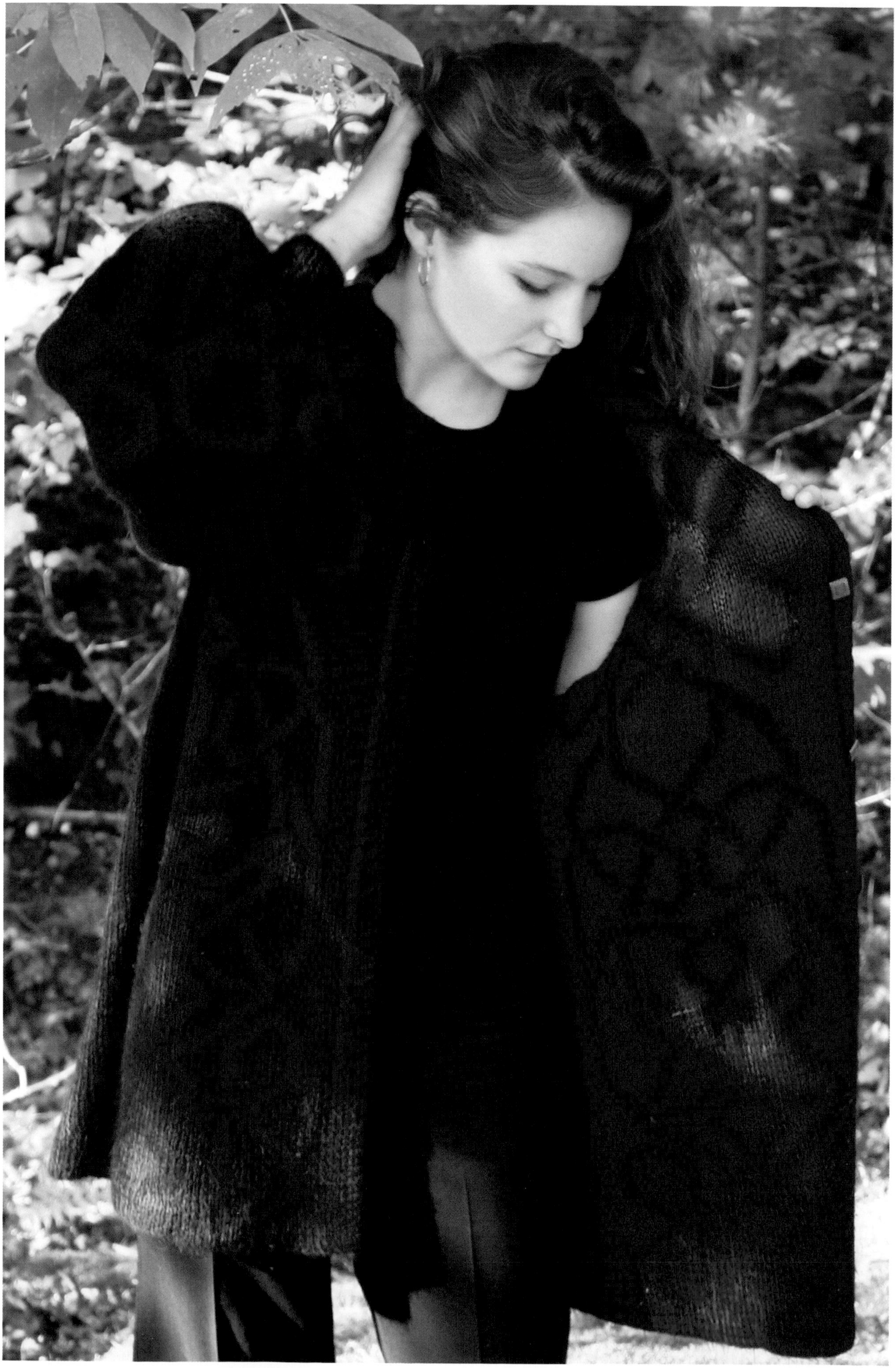

Celtic Crossroads

The Celtic Crossroads coat is my favorite; it was the first large garment I made. I feel very elegant when I wear it and people really do turn and take a second look. The coat is size large to fit me, but I have a skinny, model-looking friend and she looks wonderful in it as well.

Finished Size:

Circumference:	53"
Hem to Underarm:	25"
Armhole Depth:	10"
Sleeve length:	19"

To make this coat larger or smaller, adjust the number of plain stitches between the Celtic motifs.

Gauge: 16 DSPs and 20 rows = 4"

Materials: A lightweight mohair: 2100 yards of two colors.

Needles: 16" and 36" (or 40") circular and straight needles in size US 7, 16" circular and dp needles in size US 5, an extra circular needle in a size close to US 7 (US 4, 5, 6, or 7)

Notions: Markers, stitch holders, buttons

Body

Using larger circular needle and color A, cast on 420 stitches. That may seem like too many stitches and you think that I'm crazy or the printer made a mistake, but half of the stitches are for side A, and half are for side B.

Row 1: Using color A only, knit a single stitch, loosely tie on color B and, *byb, k1 with color A, byf, p1 with color B. Repeat from * until 1 single stitch remains, using color A only, knit the last stitch. You have 1 edge stitch, 209 DSPs, and 1 edge stitch.

Row 2: Sl 1 p'wise, *byb, k1 using color B, byf, p1 with color A. Repeat from * to last stitch, drop color B on side of your work closest to you, using color A only, knit last stitch.

Note: For the rest of this pattern, CES (Closed Edge Stitch - see *Edge Stitches* on page 14) means:
 - at the beginning of each row, sl 1 single stitch p'wise, pick up color B and twist yarns to prevent hole, continue.
 - at the end of each row, drop color B on the side of your work closest to you and, using color A only, knit the last single stitch.

Row 3: Begin following chart (begin with row 3) as follows: CES, DK to last single stitch, CES.

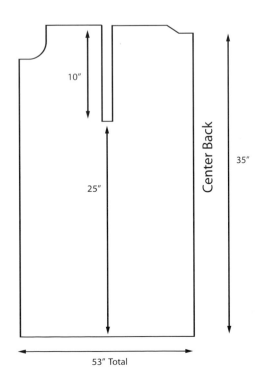

53" Total

10"

25"

Center Back

35"

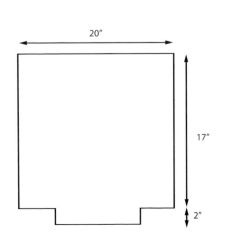

20"

17"

2"

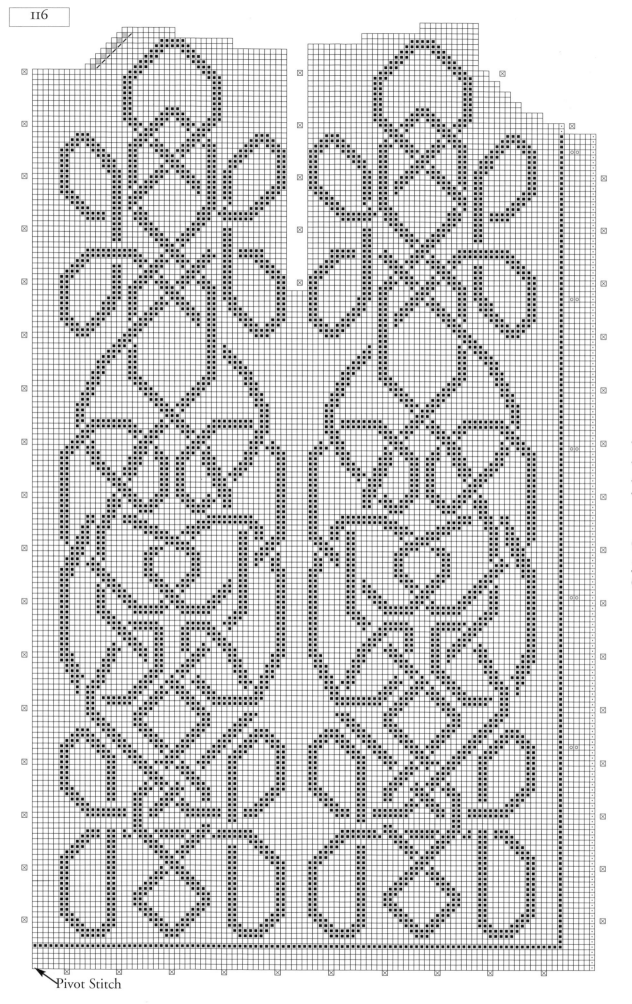

DOUBLE KNITTING

Celtic Crossroads body chart

Pivot Stitch

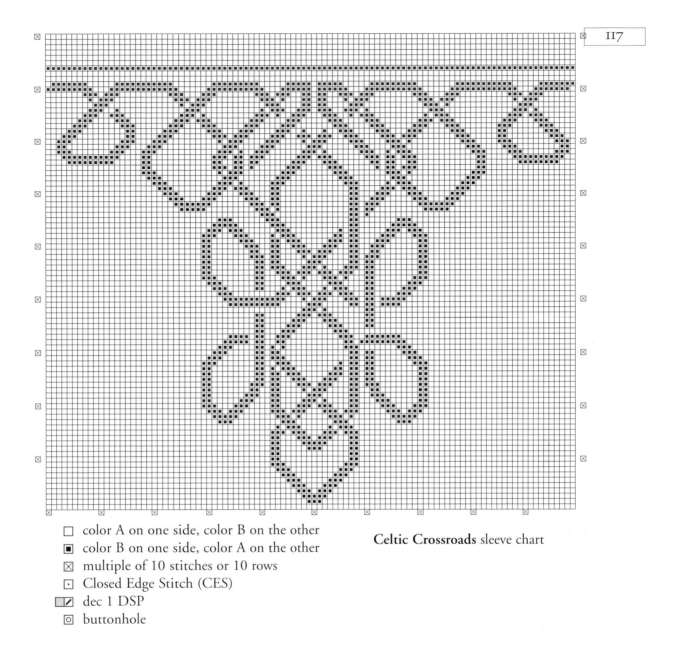

□ color A on one side, color B on the other
■ color B on one side, color A on the other
⊠ multiple of 10 stitches or 10 rows
⊡ Closed Edge Stitch (CES)
▨ dec 1 DSP
◉ buttonhole

Celtic Crossroads sleeve chart

Rows 4-128: Continue following the chart as established, making buttonholes on rows 43, 71, 99 and 127 (see below for buttonhole).

Buttonhole Rows: CES, work 2 DSPs, BO tog 2 DSPs (see *Binding Off* on page 13). Finish row, following chart, CES.

Row 129, armhole: Using another needle of same size, CES, work 53 DSPs, put 4 pairs on hold. Leave the remaining stitches on the circular needle. Turn.

First Front

Rows 130-157: At the armhole edge, you now want an Open Edge Stitch (OES - see *Edge*

Stitches on page 14). DK following the chart, making sure that the two colors are **not** twisted at the armhole edge. Work across to last stitch as established, CES. Work a buttonhole on row 155.

Row 158, neck shaping: Beginning at armhole edge, DK until 6 DSPs and edge stitch remain. Drop color B, and using color A only, *k1, p1, repeat to end of row, ending with CES. Turn.

Row 159: Sl 1 p'wise, *k2tog (a knit and a purl), psso (1 pair bound off). Repeat from * 5 more times. Twist colors A and B together and DK to end of row. Turn.

Row 160: OES, DK to end of row. Turn.

MoHAIR
celtic twist
red + violet

Second Front

Row 129: At the front edge of the coat, loosely tie on both yarns. Using a another needle, work CES, DK 53 pairs, put 4 pairs on hold. Leave the remaining stitches on the circular needle. Turn.

Rows 130-180: Work the second front exactly as you did the First Front, omitting the buttonholes. Remember to keep an OES at the armhole, and a CES at the front of the coat.

Back

Tie on both yarns at side next to the first armhole. For the back section, have an OES at both edges of the fabric.

Rows 129-170: OES, DK to end of row. Turn.

Row 171, back neck shaping: OES, work 37 DSPs (38 total). Leave remaining stitches on needle. Turn.

First Shoulder

Row 172, neck edge: Dec 1 DSP, DK to end of row. Turn.

Row 173: OES, DK to within 2 pairs of end of row, dec 1 DSP. Turn.

Row 174: Dec 1 DSP, DK to end of row. Turn.

Row 175: Work 10 DSPs and move them to a holder, DK to within 2 pairs of end, dec 1 DSP, Turn.

Row 176-178: Continue as established, adding stitches to holder as shown on chart.

Move remaining 11 DSPs to the holder.

Row 161: Work 3 DSPs. Slip these to a stitch holder so that the open end of the holder is facing the work in progress; you will add more stitches to this holder on subsequent rows. DK across row. Turn.

Row 162-175: Continue as established, moving pairs at neck edge to holder as shown on chart.

Row 176, shoulder shaping: Work 10 DSPs and move them to second holder, DK to end of row. Turn.

Row 177: DK to end of row. Turn.

Row 178: Work 11 DSPs and add them to holder, DK to end of row. Turn.

Row 179: DK to end of row.

Row 180: Move remaining 11 pairs to holder.

Second Shoulder

At front edge of coat, loosely tie on both yarns. Begin with row 172 and work exactly as you did for First Shoulder. Put 19 stitches at center back on holder.

Shoulder Seams

*Take the stitches for the front right shoulder and split them onto two needles as follows: color A stitches on one needle, color B stitches on the second needle. Repeat this process for the right shoulder stitches from the back of the coat. Using color A, either kitchener the color A shoulder stitches together, or use 3-needle BO to unite them. Turn to the other side and BO the color B stitches. Repeat from * for left shoulder stitches.

Sleeves

Work the sleeve circularly from shoulder to cuff. There are 93 rows around the sleeve opening, but the sleeves are gathered slightly. You need to pick up 100 stitches in those 93 rows (see *Pick Up vs Knit Up* on page 16).

Using a circular needle similar in size to your working size, and with side A facing, pick up 100 stitches (including 4 stitches in color A on hold) around the sleeve opening. Put these aside and turn to the color B side of the garment. Using a

DOUBLE KNITTING

second circular needle, and with side B facing, pick up 100 stitches (including 4 stitches in color B on hold) around the sleeve opening.

Round 1: Loosely tie on both yarns at the center underarm. Using a 16" needle (same size as used for body), begin DK as follows: Hold the side A stitches and side B stitches parallel. *Byb, k1 from side A needle, byf, p1 from side B needle. Repeat from * until all stitches are on one needle (100 DSPs).

Rounds 2-90: Follow the chart (begin with row 2), knitting circularly.

Row 91, decrease: Loosely tie off color B. Using a smaller 16" circular needle and color A, *k2tog (one stitch of color A, one of color B). Repeat from * until all pairs have been knitted together. Change to dp needles when necessary (100 stitches).

Row 92: *K2tog, p2tog, repeat from * (50 stitches).

Rows 93-101: Work in k1, p1 ribbing.

Bind off in ribbing.

Work second sleeve.

Collar

Pick up stitches around the neck, just as you did for the sleeves. You will need three needles again; one for color A, one for color B and the one to DK onto as you establish Double Knitting. When you get to the stitches on holders, you need to separate them onto the two needles, one for color A, and one for color B. I picked up 28 stitches from each front and 35 stitches from the back neck.

For ease of handling, I transferred all the stitches from the separate circular needles to one needle, alternating colors A and B.

Row 1: Loosely tie on both yarns. Using both colors held together as one, knit the first DSP together. Using appropriate background color (to match the side you're working on), *work 3 DSPs, dec 1 pair, repeat from * to the last pair, knit last DSP together using both yarns.

Row 2: Sl 1 p'wise, DK to within one stitch of end of row, k1 using both yarns.

Rows 3 and 4: Sl 1 p'wise, DK to within one stitch of end of row reversing colors to make a 2-row stripe, k1 using both yarns.

Row 5: Reverse colors again and work as established.

Row 6, decrease: Sl 1 p'wise, *work 5 DSPs, dec 1 DSP, repeat from * to last pair, knit last DSP together as one.

Rows 7-10: Continue as established.

Row 11, decrease: Reverse colors for a 1-row stripe and work decreases as in row 6.

Row 12: Continue as established.

Row 13: Tie off one color. Using remaining color, k all stitches.

Row 14: K2tog, *k2tog, pass first stitch over, repeat from * to end of row to bind off all stitches.

Finishing

Sew up the two sets of underarm stitches. Pull in all the loose ends. Go to the store and find the perfect buttons and sew them on both sides. Show to your friends; or better yet find someone to take you out to dinner.

Oceans to Cross

This woman's coat is in one size. It fits almost everyone. The coat is knit from the bottom hem to the armholes, then each front and the back are knit separately. The shoulders are sewn together and the sleeves are knit from the armhole down to the hem. I wanted to have dress sleeves without the ribbing. You may add a ribbed cuff, if you like; it would simply take more decreasing on the last row - then switching to one yarn and ribbing until you are happy. Instead of a ribbed neck band or collar, I made an attached scarf.

Because of the effect of the scarf ends crossing in front and then tossed back over the shoulders, I found I didn't like buttons, so I sewed on a silk-covered snap at the neck edges.

Finished Size:

Circumference: 45", allowing for overlap
Length from hem to underarm: 29"
Armhole depth: 9"

Gauge: 19 DSPs and 20 rows = 4"

Materials: 2000 yds each of 2 colors of DK weight yarn. The sample was knitted in mohair.

Needles: 16" and 29" circular needles, straight needles, and dp needles in US 6 (4 mm), an extra circular needle in a size close to US 6 (US 4, 5, 6, or 7)

Notions: 2 markers, 1 silk-covered snap

Body

The entire body is worked back and forth. On the odd-numbered rows, read the chart from right to left. On the even-numbered rows, read the chart from left to right (see *Reading Charts* on page 17).

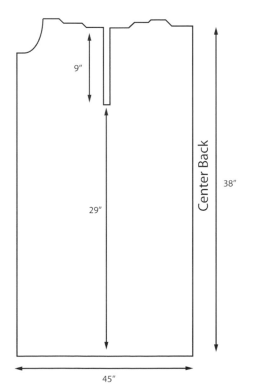

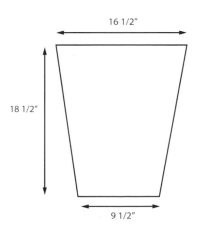

DOUBLE KNITTING

The row below is on the needles as you continue the chart

start here

Oceans To Cross body chart

continue on opposite page

DOUBLE KNITTING

Using color A, cast on 210 stitches.

Set-Up Row (not shown on chart): K and p into each stitch creating 210 DSPs (see *Establishing DSPs* on page 10). Turn.

Row 1: Sl 1 single stitch p'wise, DK 209 pairs following chart (row 1), drop color B on side closest to you, and using color A only, k a single stitch.

Note: For the rest of this pattern, CES (Closed Edge Stitch) means:
- at the beginning of each row, sl 1 single stitch p'wise, pick up color B and twist yarns to prevent hole, continue.
- at the end of each row, drop color B on the side of your work closest to you and, using color A only, knit the last single stitch.

Rows 2 - 141: CES, DK to last single stitch following chart, CES. Turn.

Row 142, armholes: CES, DK 54 pairs following chart, BO sep 4 DSPs (see *Binding Off* on page 13), DK 93 pairs, BO sep 4 DSPs, work 54 DSPs, CES. Turn.

First Front

Row 143: Using another needle, CES, DK to the first armhole. At the armhole edge, make an Open Edge Stitch (work the stitches as shown on the chart and don't twist the yarns together after you turn (see *Edge Stitches* on page 14). This makes picking up sleeve stitches neater.

Leave the remaining stitches on the circular needle and continue on the First Front only.

Row 144-180: Continue according to the chart to the neck shaping, keeping a CES at the front edge and an OES (Open Edge Stitch) at armhole edge.

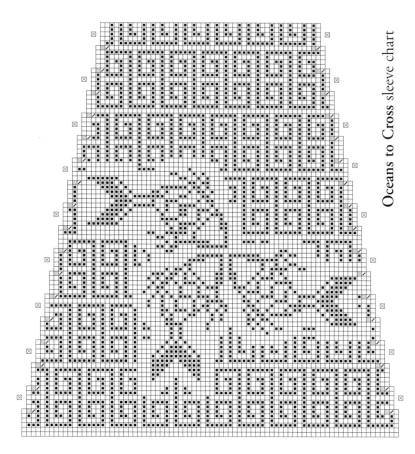

Oceans to Cross sleeve chart

- ☐ color A on one side, color B on the other
- ■ color B on one side, color A on the other
- ⊠ multiple of 10 stitches or 10 rows
- ⊡ Closed Edge Stitch (CES)
- ▱ dec 1 DSP

Row 181, neck shaping: BO edge stitch, BO tog 7 DSPs, BO sep 5 DSPs. You've bound off the edge stitch and 12 pairs. Dec 1 DSP, DK across row. Turn.

Row 181: DK to last 2 pairs, dec 1 DSPs. Turn.

Row 182: Dec 1 DSP, DK to end of row. Turn.

Rows 183-190: Continue as established, following chart.

Row 191, shoulder shaping: BO sep 11 DSPs, DK to end of row. Turn.

Row 192: DK to end of row. Turn.

Row 193: BO sep 11 stitches, DK to end of row. Turn.

Row 195: BO sep 11 stitches.

Center Back

Row 144: Starting at the armhole next to the front you just finished, tie on both yarns. Keep both sides of the back as Open Edge Stitches. Using another needle, DK to other armhole following the Body Chart. Leave the remaining stitches (Second Front) on circular needle and continue on Center Back only.

Rows 145-189: DK according to Body Chart.

Row 190, divide for neck: BO sep 11 DSPs. DK 22 pairs, dec 1 DSP. Place the next 21 DSPs on a holder. Tie on 2 more skeins of yarn. Dec 1 DSP, DK to end of row.

Row 191, first shoulder: BO sep 11 DSPs. DK 21 pairs, dec 1 DSP. Turn.

Row 192: Dec 1 DSP, DK to end of row. Turn.

Row 193: BO sep 11 DSPs. DK to end of row. Turn.

BO sep 11 stitches.

Row 191, second shoulder: Starting at the neck edge of the back, tie on both yarns. Dec 1 DSP, DK across row. Turn.

Row 192: BO sep 11 pairs, DK to last 2 pairs, dec 1 DSP. Turn.

BO sep 11 pairs.

Second Front

Row 143: Starting at armhole edge, join on both colors. Keep the armhole edge as an OES. Using another needle, DK to last stitch, CES. Turn.

Row 144-180: Continue according to the chart to the neck shaping, keeping an OES at the armhole and a CES at the front edge.

Row 182: DK to last 2 DSPs, dec 1 DSP. Turn.

Row 183-189: Continue as established, following chart.

Row 190, shoulder shaping: BO sep 11 DSPs, DK to end of row. Turn.

Row 191: DK to end of row. Turn.

Row 192: BO sep 11 DSPs, DK to end of row. Turn.

Row 193: BO sep 11 stitches.

Shoulder Seams

*Line up one of the front shoulders with the corresponding back shoulder. Using color A, sew the color A shoulder seam. Turn to the other side and sew the color B shoulder seam. Repeat from * for second shoulder.

Sleeves

The sleeves are worked in the round from the top of the sleeve to the bottom. Because you are working in the round, you now follow each line of the chart from right to left. All the sleeve decreases are made at the underarm and I like to leave one stitch on either side of the marking ring and then decrease.

Set-Up Round: On side A at the center underarm, tie on color A. Using a spare circular needle, knit up 82 stitches around armhole. Leave this dangling. Turn the garment over and, at the same center underarm, tie on color B. Using another spare circular needle, knit up 82 stitches around side B.

Round 1: Using the US 6 circular needle, DK around sleeve as follows: Byb, k1 from front needle, byf, p1 from back needle. After you work 82 pairs, all stitches are on the circular needle. Pm.

Round 2: Begin following chart (start with row 2) working in the round.

Rounds 3-87: DK as established following chart. When the sleeve becomes too small for the circular needle, change to DPs.

On about round 50, I tried on the coat to see how long the sleeves would be and found that they were almost long enough. If you are taller, you can work the entire sleeve chart. Once the sleeve is the length you want, BO together all stitches. Knit second sleeve.

Neck Scarf

Using one of the spare circular needles, and starting at the top of the front border, pick up 49 stitches around the neck edge on side A (see *Pick Up vs Knit Up* on page 16).

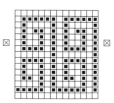

Oceans to Cross scarf chart

Turn garment over and, using another needle, pick up 49 stitches on side B. Using a 24" US 6 needle, cast on 100 stitches. Turn. Work k1, p1 ribbing to end of row. Put this section aside.

Using another US 6 needle, cast on 100 stitches. Turn. Work k1, p1 ribbing to end of row. Turn.

Set-Up Row: Work 5 stitches in ribbing. Loosely tie on color B. *Byb, using color A, k the first stitch and leave it on the left-hand needle, byf, p the same stitch and remove it from the left-hand needle, repeat from * across to end of row. Don't turn.

Work across the 49 color A neck stitches and the 49 color B neck stitches as follows: hold the side A stitches and side B stitches parallel. *Byb, k1 from side A needle, byf, p1 from side B needle. Repeat from * to end of 49 DSPs.

Pick up the 100-stitch piece you put aside and work across it, making the first 95 stitches into DSPs (as above). Using color A only, work last 5 stitches in ribbing. Turn.

You now have 5 ribbing stitches, 239 DSPs, and 5 ribbing stitches.

Row 1: Work 5 stitches in ribbing. Begin following chart (start with row 1) and repeat the 14-stitch chart (row 1 is plain) until 5 stitches remain, using color A only, work 5 stitches in ribbing. Turn.

Rows 2-16: Continue as established, following chart.

Row 17 (not shown on chart): Work 5 stitches in ribbing, drop color B and, using color A only, *k2tog the next 2 stitches (one k and one p), p2tog the next 2 stitches (one k and one p), repeat from * to last 5 stitches, work 5 stitches in ribbing. Turn.

Bind off loosely.

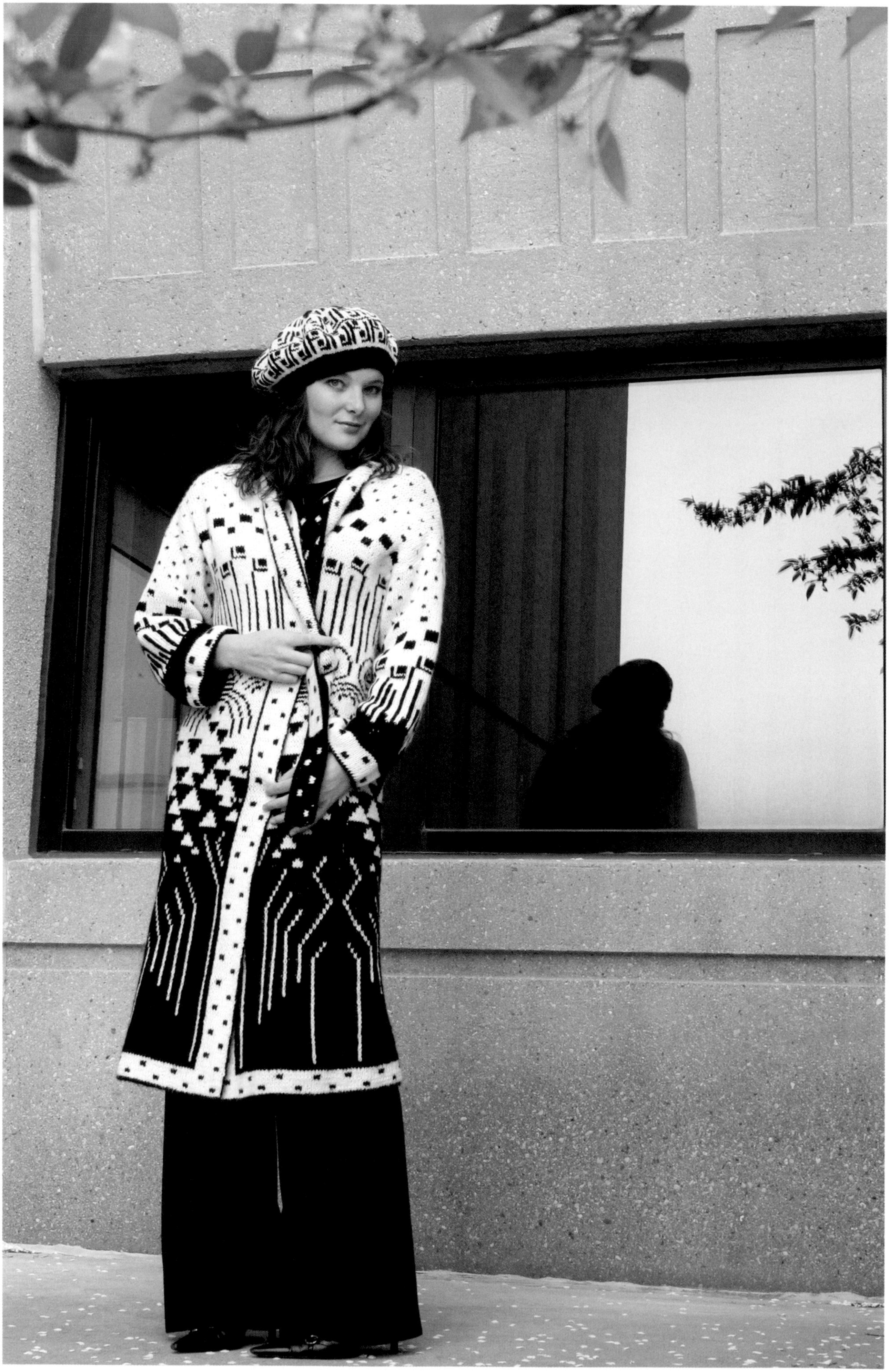

Art Deco Coat

This coat is shaped like the previous coat, *Oceans to Cross*, with the neck scarf tied at the throat. The black and white sets off the art deco theme nicely.

Finished Size:

Circumference: 45", allowing for overlap
Length from hem to underarm: 35"
Armhole depth: 8.5"

Gauge: 19 DSPs and 24 rows = 4"

Materials: 1800 yds each of 2 colors of sport weight yarn.

Needles: 16" and 29" circular needles, straight needles, and dp needles in US 4 (3.5 mm), an extra circular needle in a size close to US 4 (US 3, 4, 5, or 6)

Notions: 2 markers, sewing needle, 1 silk-covered snap

Body

Using 29" circular needle and two strands of color A held together, cast on 213 stitches. Turn.

Set-up Row: Loosely tie on color B and cut off one of the color A strands. Sl 1 DSP. * Byb, k1 with color B, byf, p1 with color A. Repeat from * until 1 pair remains. Using color A only, knit the last DSP together. You have 1 edge stitch, 211 DSPs, and 1 edge stitch. This sets up Closed Edge Stitches (CESs - see *Edge Stitches* on page 14).

Note: For the rest of this pattern, CES means:

- at the beginning of each row, slip a single stitch p'wise, pick up color B and twist yarns to prevent hole, continue.

- at the end of each row, drop color B on the side of your work closest to you and, using color A only, knit the last single stitch.

Row 1: Begin following chart (begin with row 1) as follows: CES, DK following chart to Pivot Stitch, then, reading the chart from left to right, repeat the pattern back to the beginning, CES. Turn.

Rows 2-210: Continue as established following chart.

Row 211, armholes: Using another needle, CES, DK 54 pairs, put 4 pairs on hold. Leave the remaining stitches on the circular needle. Turn.

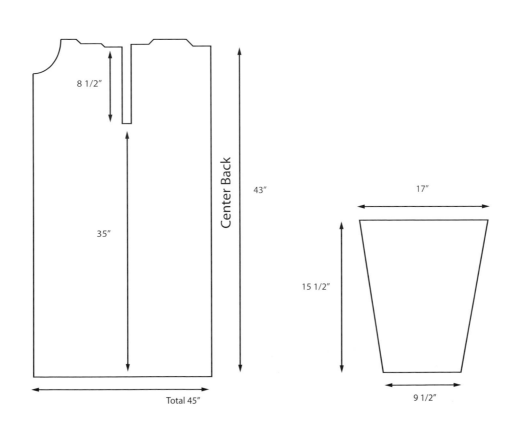

First Front

Rows 212-249: Work as established, keeping a CES at the front edge and an OES (Open Edge Stitch - see *Edge Stitches* on page 14) at armhole edge. Turn.

Row 250, neck shaping: Beginning at armhole edge, DK until 11 DSPs and edge stitch remain. Drop color B, and using color A only, k each knit stitch and p each purl stitch. Turn.

Row 251: Sl 1 p'wise, *k2tog and bind off one DSP. Repeat from * until edge stitch and 11 DSPs are bound off. DK to end of row.

Row 252: DK to within 3 pairs of end, dec 1 DSP, work 1 DSP. Turn.

Row 253: Work 1 DSP, dec 1 DSP, DK to end of row. Turn.

Rows 254-259: Continue as established, following chart.

Row 260: BO sep 11 DSPs, DK to within 3 pairs of end, dec 1 DSP, work 1 pair. Turn.

Row 261: Work 1 DSP, dec 1 DSP, DK to end of row. Turn.

Row 262: BO sep 11 DSPs, DK to end of row. Turn.

BO sep 11 DSPs.

Second Front

Row 211: At the front edge of the coat, loosely tie on both yarns. Using another US 4 needle, CES, work 54 DSPs, put 4 pairs on hold. Leave the remaining stitches on the circular needle. Turn.

Rows 212-262: Work the second front exactly as you did the First Front. Remember to keep an OES at the armhole edge and a CES at the front edge.

Back

Tie on both yarns at side next to the first armhole. For the back section, have an OES at both edges of the fabric.

Rows 211-258: DK to end of row. Turn.

First Shoulder

Row 259, back neck shaping: Work 37 DSPs, put next 23 DSPs on hold. Turn.

Row 260, neck edge: Dec 1 DSP, DK to end of row. Turn.

Row 261: BO sep 11 DSPs, DK until 2 pairs remain, dec 1 DSP. Turn.

Row 262: Dec 1 DSP, DK to end of row. Turn.

Row 263: BO sep 11 DSPs, DK until 2 pairs remain, dec 1 DSP. Turn.

Row 264: Dec 1 DSP, DK to end of row. Turn.

Row 265: BO sep 11 DSPs.

Second Shoulder

Rows 259-265: At the front edge of the coat, loosely tie on both yarns. Work the second shoulder exactly as you did the first shoulder.

Shoulder Seams

*Take the stitches for the front right shoulder and split them onto two dp needles as follows: color A stitches on one needle, color B stitches on the second needle. Repeat this process for the right shoulder stitches from the back of the coat. Using color A, weave or sew together the color A shoulders. Turn to the other side and weave or sew the color B stitches. Repeat from * for left shoulder stitches.

Sleeves

The sleeves are worked in the round from the top of the sleeve to the bottom. Because you are working in the round, you now follow each line of the chart from right to left. All the sleeve decreases are made at the underarm and I like to leave one stitch on either side of the marking ring and then decrease.

Set-Up Round: Loosely tie on color A at the center underarm, just after the 4 DSPs that are on hold. Using a spare circular needle (similar in size to your working size), and with side A facing, Knit Up 78 stitches around the sleeve opening.

When you get back to the 4 DSPs that are on hold, knit the 4 color A stitches, but leave the 4 color B stitches of the other side. Put these 82 color A stitches aside and turn to the color B side of the garment.

Loosely tie on color B at the center underarm, just after the 4 color B stitches that are on hold. Using a second circular needle, and with side B facing, Knit Up 78 stitches around the sleeve opening. Knit into the 4 color B stitches that are on hold at the underarm (82 stitches).

Round 1: Using a 16" US 4 needle, begin Double Knitting as follows: Hold the side A stitches and side B stitches parallel. *Byb, using color A, k1 from side A needle, byf, using color B, p1 from side B needle. Repeat from * until all stitches are on one needle - 82 DSPs.

Round 2: Begin following chart (start with row 2). DK entire round.

Rounds 3-8: Repeat row 2.

Round 9: Work 1 DSP, using color A only, k2tog the next 2 knit stitches, using B only, p2tog the next 2 purl stitches. DK to within 3 pairs of marker. Using color A only, k2tog the next 2 knit stitches, using color B only, p2tog the next 2 purl stitches, DK last stitch.

Art Deco chart, upper portion

The row below is on the needles as you continue the chart

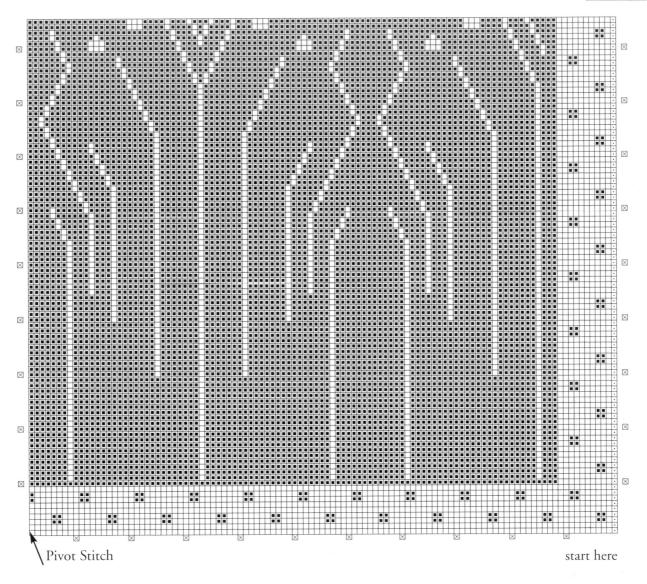

Pivot Stitch

start here

Art Deco chart, lower portion

Rounds 10-13: DK entire round.

Round 14: Repeat round 9.

Rounds 15-89: Repeat rounds 10-14 fifteen times more. When the sleeve becomes too small for the circular needle, change to DPs. On about round 60, try on the coat to see how long the sleeves are; adjust as necessary.

Final Round: Once the sleeve is the length you want, BO tog all stitches.

Neck Scarf

Setting Up for Scarf: Using one of the spare circular needles, and starting at the top of the front border on side A, Pick Up (not Knit Up) 12 stitches, then move the 25 color A stitches (on hold at back of neck) onto needle, then pick up 12 more stitches. Turn garment over and, using another circular, do the same thing for side B. Using a US 4 straight needle and two strands of color A, cast on 100 stitches. Turn, cut one strand of color A and loosely tie on color B. *Byb, using color B, k1, byf, using color A, p1. Repeat from * to end of row (100 DSPs). Set this aside. Using another US 4 needle and two strands of color A, cast on 100 stitches. Turn, cut one strand of color A and loosely tie on color B. *Byb, using color B, k1, byf, using color A, p1. Repeat from * to end of row (100 DSPs). Turn.

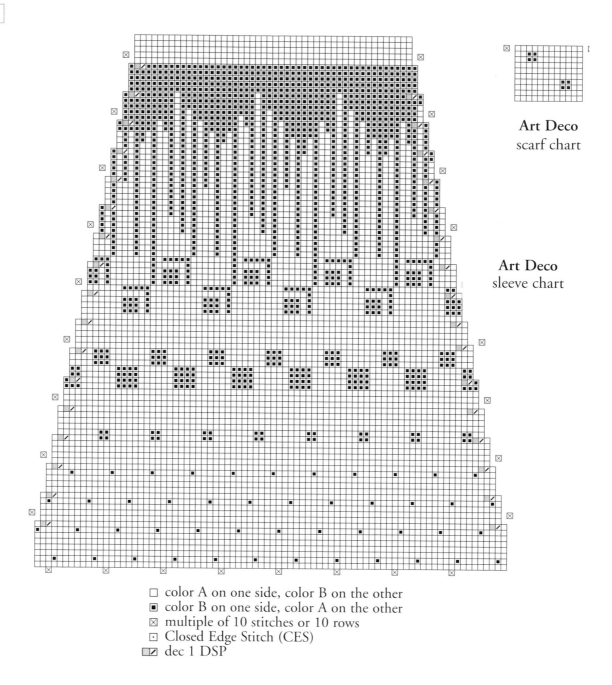

Art Deco
scarf chart

Art Deco
sleeve chart

□ color A on one side, color B on the other
■ color B on one side, color A on the other
☒ multiple of 10 stitches or 10 rows
⊡ Closed Edge Stitch (CES)
◪ dec 1 DSP

Row 1: Sl 1, *byb, using color A, k1, byf, using color B, p1. Repeat from * across 100-stitch piece. Pick up coat, and with side A facing, continue to DK around the neck edge (49 DSPs). Work across second 100-stitch piece until 1 DSP remains, using color A only, k last DSP together as one stitch. Turn. You now have 1 edge stitch, 247 DSPs, 1 edge stitch.

Rows 2-10: Follow appropriate row on chart, working the 12-stitch repeat 20 times, plus 7 stitches of one more repeat as follows: CES, work 247 DSPs, CES stitch. Turn.

Row 11 (not shown on chart): Using color A only, *k1, p1. Repeat from * across entire row. Turn.

Binding Off: Sl 1 knitwise, *k2tog, BO, repeat from * across row.

Finishing:
You can either crochet around the entire coat or apply I-Cord. I began where the scarf ends meet the neck and worked out to the front edge, down the front, across the bottom, up the other front and onto the neck. I also worked around the bottom of each sleeve. Option: put a silk snap where the fronts overlap to hold the coat together nicely.

DOUBLE KNITTING

Art Deco Tam

Materials 3.5 oz (100 gm) skein of sport weight yarn in two colors: white (color A) and black (color B).

Needles US 4 (3.5 mm) 16-inch circular, US 4 (3.5mm) dpns

You have 144 pairs in the hat, and an 8-stitch repeat, so everything works out perfectly.

Directions: Using 16-inch needle and color B, cast on 100 sts. Place a marker and join, being careful not to twist the stitches over the needle.

Rounds 1-9: Work k1, p1 ribbing.

Round 10, increase: Work 7 sts in ribbing, inc 1, *rib 2, inc 1*, repeat from * to * 43 times, rib 7 (144 sts).

Round 11: Knit.

Round 12, set-up for DK: Still using color B, knit into the front and back (kfb) of every stitch (288 sts, or 144 DSPs).

Round 13: Tie on color A and *Byb, k1 with color A, byf, p1 with color B. Repeat from * to end of round.

Rounds 14 & 15: *Byb, k1 with color A, byf, p1 with color B. Repeat from * to end of round.

Rounds 16-27: Work in DK, following Chart 1.

Rounds 28-37: Work rows 1-10 of Chart 1 again.

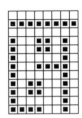

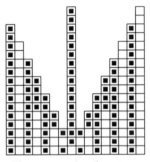

Chart 1

Chart 2, top-shaping

Round 38, decrease: Using color A for the k sts, and color B for the p sts, DK 8 pairs, dec 1 DSP, *work 2 DSPs, dec 1 DSP* repeat from * to * until 10 pairs remain, DK 10 pairs (112 DSPs).

Round 39: *Byb, k1 with color A, byf, p1 with color B. Repeat from * to end of round.

Rounds 40-42: Work in DK, following Chart 2.

Round 43: *DK 6 pairs, dec 1 DSP, work 1 pair, dec 1 DSP, DK 5 pairs, repeat from * to end of round (98 DSPs).

Rounds 44-56: Continue, following chart and decreasing as shown every other row. Change to dpns when necessary (14 DSPs)

Round 57: *Byb, k2tog with color B, byf, p2tog with color A. Repeat from * to end of round.

Finishing
Cut both yarns, leaving a long tail. Thread each onto needle and run through the remaining sts on each side separately. Pull up and weave in ends. Wear.

DOUBLE KNITTING

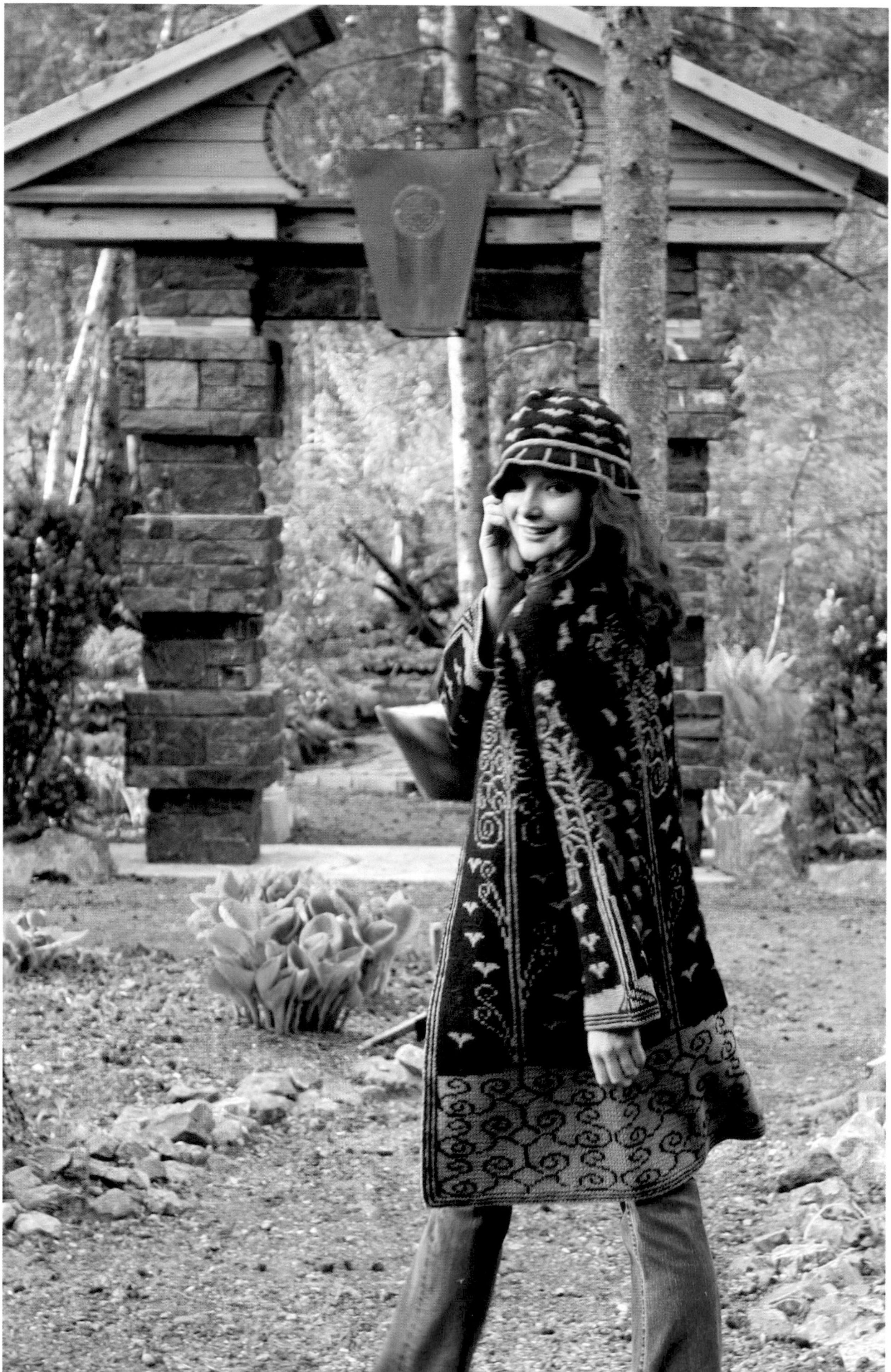

Central Park
Coat & Cloche

This charming "art nouveau" clutch coat with it's own cloche knits up quickly at 5 stitches to the inch: any sport yarn in any two colors. To make a larger size change to worsted weight yarn and a larger needle.

Finished Size:
>   Circumference: 42"
>   Length from hem to underarm: 30"
>   Armhole depth: 9"

Gauge: 20 DSPs and 25 rows = 4"

Materials: 1500 yds each of 2 colors of sport weight yarn. I used Brown Sheep Nature Spun Sport, colors Latte and Bulldog Blue.

Needles: 16" and 29" circular needles, straight needles, and dp needles in US 3 (3 mm), an extra circular needle in a size close to US 3 (US 2, 3, 4, or 5)

Notions: Stitch markers, 2 buttons

Body

The entire body is worked back and forth. On the odd-numbered rows, read the chart from right to left. On the even-numbered rows, read the chart from left to right (see *Reading Charts* on page 17).

Using 29" circular needle two strands of color A held together, cast on 210 stitches. Turn.

Set-up Row: Loosely tie on color B and cut off one of the color A strands. Sl 1 single stitch. *Byb, k1 with color B, byf, p1 with color A. Repeat from * until a single stitch remains, using color A only, k1. You have 1 edge stitch, 209 DSPs, and 1 edge stitch. This sets up Closed Edge Stitches (CESs) at both edges of the coat (see *Edge Stitches* on page 14). This is Row 1 of the chart.

Sleeves

The sleeves are worked from the top of the sleeve to the hem. Work them back and forth until you join in the stitches on hold at the underarm, then knit in the round. When working in the round, follow each line of the chart from right to left (see *Reading Charts* on page 17). All the sleeve decreases are made at the underarm and I like to leave one stitch on either side of the marking ring and then decrease.

Set-Up Row: On side A at the underarm and next to the 5 pairs on hold, tie on color A. Using a spare circular needle, knit up 81 stitches around armhole (see *Pick Up vs Knit Up* on page 16). Leave this dangling. Turn the garment over and, at the same center underarm, tie on color B. Using another spare circular needle, knit up 81 stitches around side B.

Row 1: Using the US 3 circular needle, DK around sleeve as follows: *Byb, k1 from front needle, byf, p1 from back needle, repeat from * until 1 pair remains. Slip the 5 pairs that are on hold to a dp needle. Knit tog the last color A stitch from sleeve with the first color A stitch from the dp needle, purl tog the corresponding color B stitches. Turn.

Row 2: DK around sleeve following chart until 1 pair remains. Knit together the last color A stitch from sleeve with next color A stitch from dp needle, purl together the corresponding color B stitches.

Rows 3-5: Repeat round 2.

Round 6: Place marker at underarm and join the sleeve into a circle. DK around following chart.

Rounds 7-135: DK around following chart, decreasing where indicated.

Round 136: Cut color B and, using color A only, *k1, p1, repeat from * around sleeve.

K2tog, *k2tog, BO, repeat from * around sleeve.

Hint: Try on the coat before binding off the sleeve. If the sleeve is too short, continue in the striped band until you have a length you like.

Knit second sleeve.

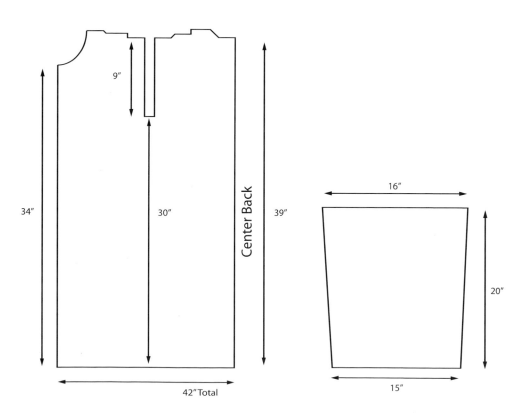

34" 9" 30" Center Back 39" 42" Total

16" 20" 15"

Finishing

Neck: Start at either side and move the 1 edge stitch and 13 DSPs to a circular needle. Using 2 spare needles, pick up 14 stitches between these stitches and center back. Pick up 14 stitches from center back to other front, then add on the 13 DSPs and edge stitch from the second holder. You may need to rearrange the stitches to get them into the proper order for DK.

Work CESs and stripe patterns as established and DK 5 rows of the opposite color (use color B on side A, and use color A on side B). Cut and tie off color B. Using color A only, *k1, p1 across row.

On the next row, slip the first stitch, *k2tog, pass stitch over, repeat from * binding off the entire row.

Make a loop for the button at the top neck edge, either by crochet or buttonhole stitch. Sew a button on each side so the coat may be reversed.

Cloche

Using 16" circular needle and two strands of color A held together, cast on 99 stitches. PM and join into a circle to knit in the round. Cut and tie off one strand of color A and tie on color B.

Rounds 1-49: DK according to chart, decreasing where indicated - 5 DSPs remaining.

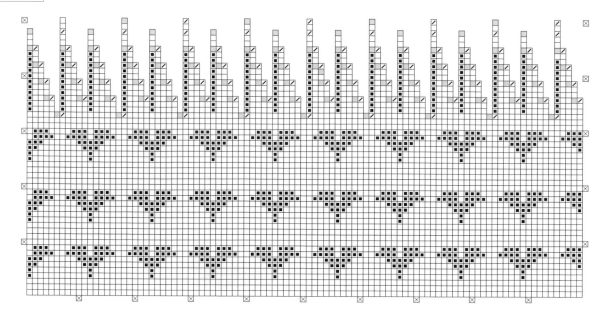

Central Park cloche chart

Run a length of color A through the 5 color A stitches, and a length of color B through the 5 color B stitches. Pull ends taut and tie off.

The Brim: On side A, using a spare circular needle, knit up 90 stitches around brim. Let the needle dangle; turn the hat to the other side and tie on color B. Using another spare needle, knit up 90 stitches around side B.

Round 1: Pm. Using the US 3 circular needle, DK around sleeve as follows: *Byb, k1 from front needle, byf, p1 from back needle, repeat from * around hat.

Continue: Make a stripe below each bird and between each 2 birds. Work two rows, then increase 2 stitches between each 2 stripes. Work 2 more rows and increase 1 stitch between each 2 stripes. Work until 12 rows are completed. Cut and tie off color B. Using color A only, k and p each stitch around.
Binding off: K2tog, *k2og, pass stitch over, repeat from * around binding off all stitches.

Finishing

With opposite color, knit up stitches along the seam where the brim meets the hat and apply I-Cord, making the ends longer so you can tie a decorative knot.

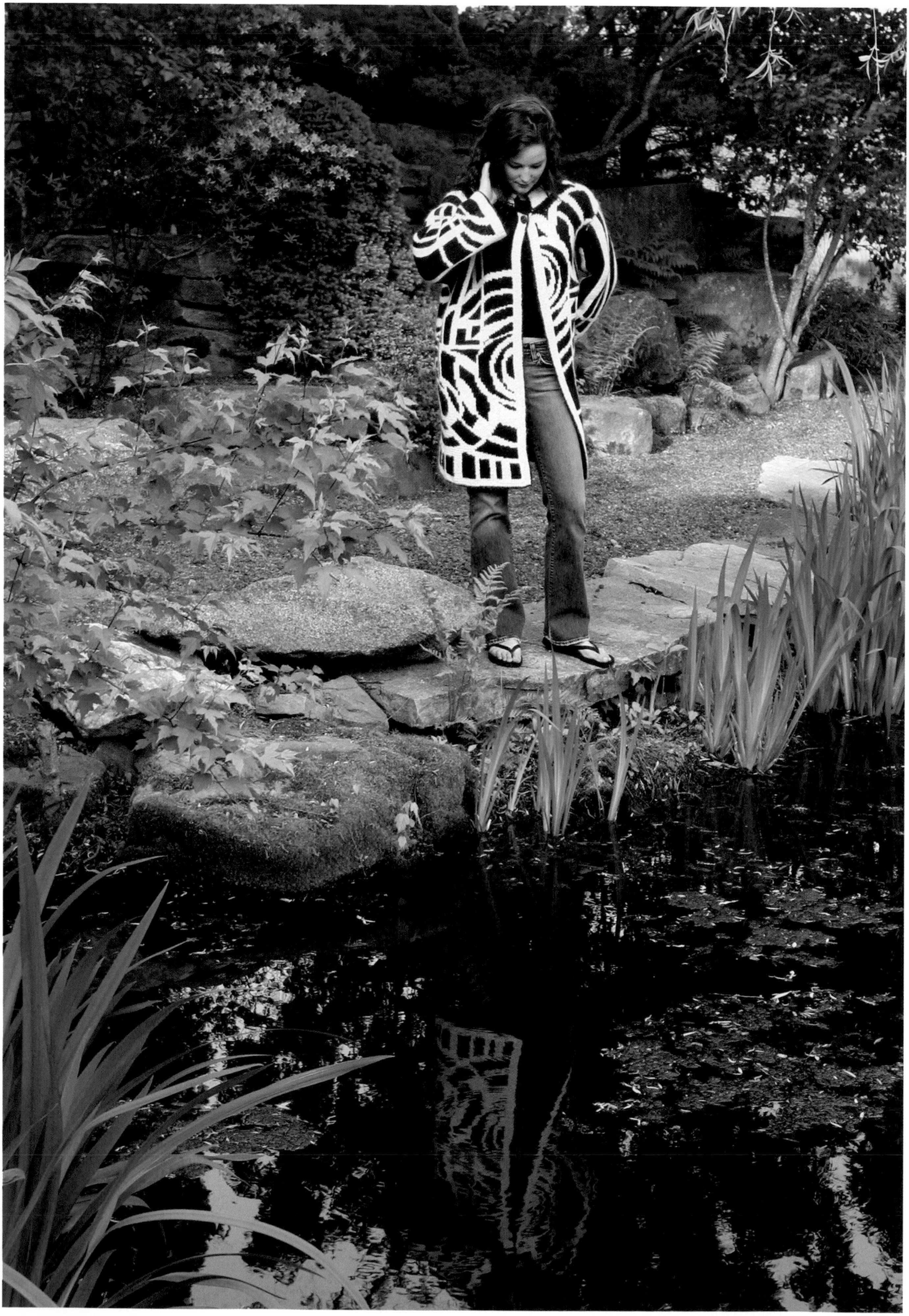

Crop Circles

Finished Size:
    Circumference: 52"
    Length from hem to underarm: 29"
    Armhole depth: 8"
    Overall length: 37"

Materials: 1100 yards each of two colors of worsted weight wool.

Gauge: 16 DSPs and 22 rows = 4"

Needles: 16" and 29" circular needles and dp needles in US 4 (3.5 mm), two extra circular needles in a size close to US 4 (US 2, 3, 4, or 5)

Notions: Stitch markers, 2 buttons, crochet hook

Body

The entire body is worked back and forth. On the odd-numbered rows, read the chart from right to left. On the even-numbered rows, read the chart from left to right (see *Reading Charts* on page 17).

Using 29" circular needle and one strand of color A, cast on 210 stitches. Turn.

Set-Up Row: Using color A, establish DSPs by knitting and purling into each stitch (see *Establishing DSPs* on page 10).

Row 1: Sl 1 p'wise, loosely tie on color B and, *byb, k1 with color A, byf, p1 with color B. Repeat to last single stitch (not pair) and k1 with color A. This establishes CESs (Closed Edge Stitches - see *Edge Stitches* on page 14). Turn.

Note: For the rest of this pattern, CES (Closed Edge Stitch) means:
- at the beginning of each row, sl 1 single stitch purlwise, pick up color B and twist yarns to prevent hole, continue.
- at the end of each row, drop color B on side of work closest to you and, using color A only, knit last single stitch.

Row 2: CES, k1 with color B, byf p1 with color A, repeat from * to last single stitch, CES. Turn.

Rows 3-160: CES, DK following chart to last single stitch, CES. Turn.

Row 161, armholes: CES, DK 46 pairs following chart. Turn. Leave the remaining stitches on the circular needle and continue on First Front only.

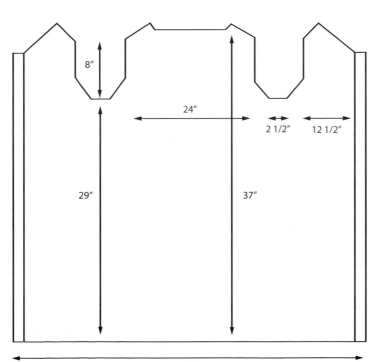

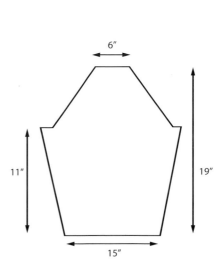

Double Knitting

The row below is on the needles as you continue the chart

Crop Circles body chart, upper portion

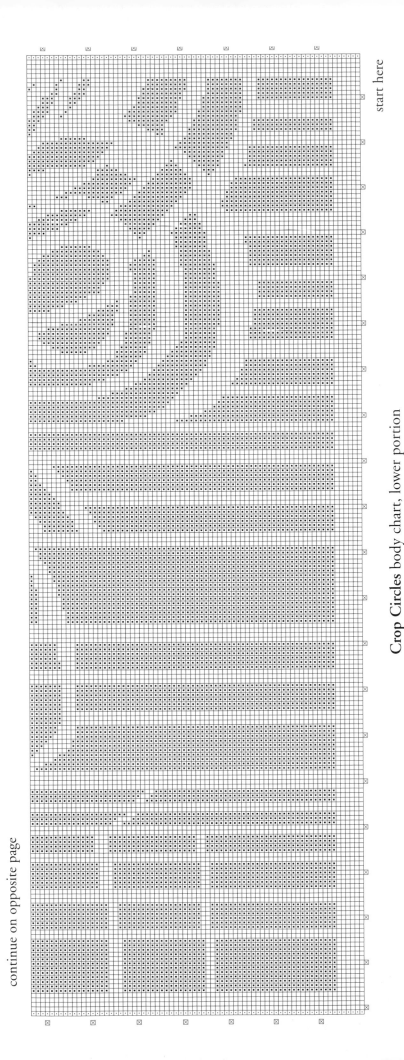

Crop Circles body chart, lower portion

start here

continue on opposite page

First Front

Row 162: Keep an Open Edge Stitch (OES - see *Edge Stitches* on page 14) at the armhole edge and a CES at the front edge. Using another needle, DK 1 pair, dec 1 DSP (see *Decreasing DSPs* on page 13), DK to last single stitch, CES. Turn.

Rows 163-193: Work as established following chart, decreasing where indicated.

Row 194: DK until 4 pairs and edge stitch remain. Drop color B and, using color A only, *k1, p1, repeat from * 4 times, CES.

Row 195, neck shaping: Using color A only, BO edge stitch and BO tog 4 DSPs (see *Binding Off* on page 13). Pick up color B and continue DK across row. Turn.

Row 196: DK to within 4 pairs of end of row, dec 1 DSP, work last 2 DSPs. Turn.

Row 197: DK 2 pairs, dec 1 DSP, DK to end of row. Turn.

Rows 198-203: Continue as established, decreasing as shown.

Row 204, shoulder shaping: BO sep 8 DSPs, DK to end of row. Turn.

Row 205: DK to end of row. Turn.

Row 206: BO sep 8 DSPs, DK to end of row. Turn.

Row 207: DK to end of row. Turn. BO sep 8 DSPs.

DOUBLE KNITTING

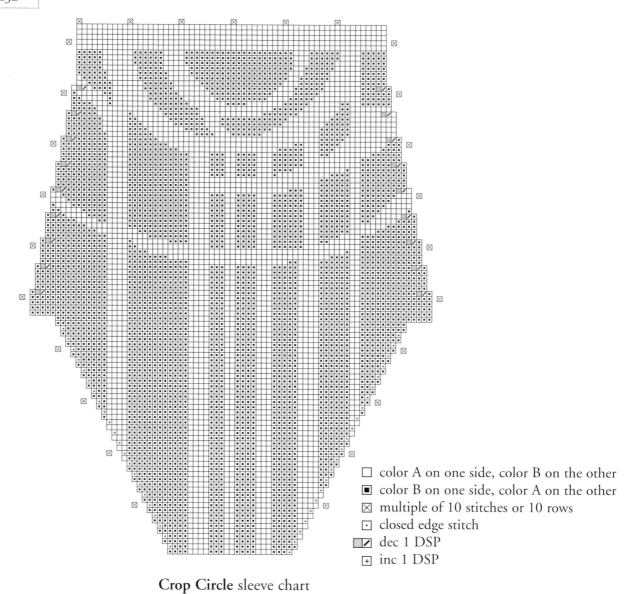

□ color A on one side, color B on the other
■ color B on one side, color A on the other
⊠ multiple of 10 stitches or 10 rows
· closed edge stitch
▨ dec 1 DSP
⊞ inc 1 DSP

Crop Circle sleeve chart

Center Back

Row 161: Starting at the armhole next to the front you just finished, put 10 DSPs on hold. Tie on both yarns and work 97 DSPs. Turn. Leave the remaining stitches (second front) on circular needle and continue with another needle on Center Back only. Keeping OESs on both edges.

Rows 162-202: Continue as established, decreasing as shown. Turn.

Row 203, first shoulder: Work 27 DSPs. Turn.

Row 204: Work 1 DSP, dec 1 DSP, DK to end of row. Turn.

Row 205: BO sep 8 DSPs. DK to within 3 pairs of end, dec 1 DSP, work final pair. Turn.

Row 206: Work 1 DSP, dec 1 DSP, DK to end of row. Turn.

Row 207: BO sep 8 DSPs. DK to end of row. Turn.

Row 208: DK to end of row. Turn.

BO sep 8 DSPs.

Second Shoulder

Row 203: Starting at neck edge of back, tie on both yarns. BO sep 25 DSPs. DK to end of row. Turn.

Row 204: BO sep 8 DSPs, DK to within 3 pairs of end, dec 1 DSP, work final pair. Turn.

Row 205: Work 1 DSP, dec 1 DSP, DK to end of row. Turn.

Row 206: BO sep 8 DSPs, DK to within 3 pairs of end, dec 1 DSP, work final DSP. Turn.

Row 207: DK to end of row. Turn.

BO sep 8 DSPs.

Second Front

Row 161: Starting at the front edge of the coat, tie on both yarns. CES, DK 46 pairs. Put remaining 10 pairs on hold. Turn.

Rows 162-207: Work exactly as you did the First Front, keeping an OES at the armhole edge and a CES at front edge.

Shoulder Seams

*Line up one of the front shoulders with the corresponding back shoulder. Using color A, sew the color A shoulder seam. Turn to the other side and sew the color B shoulder seam. Repeat from * for second shoulder.

Sleeves

The sleeves are worked from the top of the sleeve to the hem. Work them back and forth until you join in the stitches on hold at the underarm, then knit in the round. All the sleeve decreases are made at the underarm and I like to leave one stitch on either side of the marking ring and then decrease.

Set-Up Row: On side A, at the underarm and next to the 10 pairs on hold, and using a spare needle, pick up 68 stitches around armhole (34 stitches before shoulder and 34 stitches after shoulder).

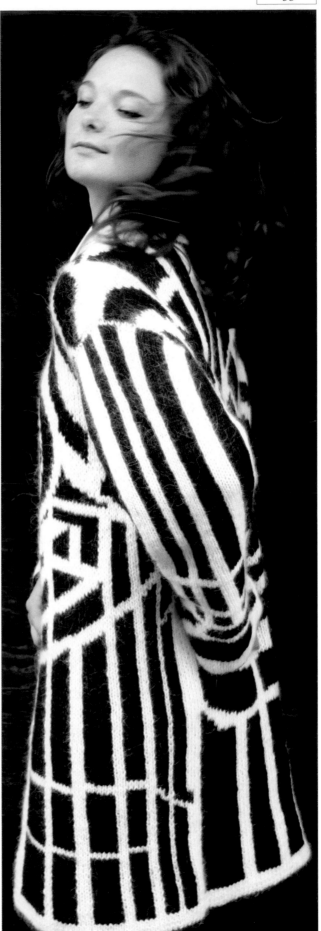

See the *Pick Up vs Knit Up* on page 16 for more information. Leave this needle dangling. Turn the garment over and, starting at the same place and using another spare circular needle, pick up 68 stitches around side B. Leave all these stitches on the spare needles, because you will be picking them up one-by-one at the end of each row as you begin the sleeve.

Row 1: Start at the shoulder seam and count down 12 pairs on each side. Tie on both yarns and, using the larger circular needle, work 24 DSPs as follows: *Byb, k1 from front needle, byf, p1 from back needle, repeat from * following color pattern on chart. Turn.

Row 2: DK across sleeve, then work 1 pair from spare needle on other side. You are adding in 1 new pair at the end of this row. Turn.

Rows 3-45: DK across row following chart, adding 1 pair from spare needle at the end of the row. Turn.

Row 46, underarm: DK across row following chart, work 10 stitches from holder at underarm.

Round 47: Join sleeves into a circle (78 DSPs) and continue working in the round following chart. Place marker at center underarm to mark beginning of round.

Rounds 48-102: DK entire round as established, decreasing where indicated.

Round 103, not shown on chart: Drop color B and, using color A only, *k1, p1, repeat from * around.

Round 104: K2tog, *k2tog, pass first stitch over, repeat from * around.

Knit second sleeve.

Neck Band

With a spare needle and working on side A only, pick up 82 stitches, including the edge stitches. Using another spare needle and working on side B, pick up 80 stitches. Slip these onto your working needle in A, B, A, B order. Loosely tie on both yarns and begin DK, working CES with color A on both edges.

Rows 1-4: CES, DK to within single stitch of end of row, CES.

Row 5: CES, work 16 DSPs, dec 1 pair, work 16 DSPs, dec 1 pair, work 8 DSPs, dec 1 pair, work 16 DSP, dec 1 pair, work 16 DSPs, CES.

Rows 6-7: CES, DK to within single stitch of end of row, CES.

Row 8: CES, DK across, decreasing every 10th pair.

Rows 9-10: CES, DK to within single stitch of end of row, CES.

Row 11: CES, DK across row, dec every 5th pair.

Rows 12-13: CES, DK to within single stitch of end of row, CES.

Row 14: Drop color B and, using color A only, *k1, p1, repeat from * to end of row.

Row 15: K2tog, *k2tog, pass first stitch over, repeat from * around.

Finishing

Using a crochet hook, pull all loose yarns into the center of the fabric. Wash by hand and block on the floor on towels, pulling the armholes and sleeves into shape. Find two beautiful buttons and sew on over a large snap on each side. Wear on a cold day.

DOUBLE KNITTING

M'Lou Baber began working in the medium of Double Knitting in the early 1990s.
Her designs and techniques have been published in *Threads* and *Interweave Knits* magazines
as well as in the books, *Great Knits* and *Sweaters from Camp*.
Throughout her life, M'Lou has been involved in a number of artistic disciplines,
including silversmithing, painting, and dressmaking.
She has exhibited at juried shows around the country and has received
several awards for her watercolors.
M'Lou spends much of her time teaching workshops, which - when she isn't knitting
or painting - is her most rewarding occupation.
M'Lou lives in Nampa, Idaho.

BIBLIOGRAPHY

Baber, M'Lou Linsert. "Twice as Nice." Interweave Knits, Winter 1997 (vol II, no. 4): 19-27.

    Sweaters From Camp. Pittsville: Schoolhouse Press, 2000.

Compton, Rae. The Illustrated Dictionary of Knitting. Loveland: Interweave Press, 1988.

    The Complete Book of Traditional Knitting. New York: Charles Scribner's Sons, 1983.

Dawson, Pam. Illustrated Guide to Knitting. New York: Monarch Press, 1977.

Dandanell, Grigitta and Danielsson, Ulla. Twined Knitting. Loveland: Interweave Press, 1989.

Gibson-Roberts, Priscilla A. Knitting in the Old Way. Loveland: Interweave Press, 1985.

Greenleaf, Barbara Kaye. America Fever. New York: Four Winds Press, 1970.

Korach Alice., ed. Knitting Around the World. Newtown: Taunton Press, 1993.

Maisel, Albert Q. They All Chose America. New York: Thomas Nelson & Sons, 1955.

Macdonald, Anne. No Idle Hands: The Social History of American Knitting. New York: Ballantine Books, 1988.

McCalls. McCall's Needlework Treasury. New York: Random House, 1964.

Neighbors, Jane F. Reversible Two-Color Knitting. New York: Charles Scribner's Sons, 1974.

Norbury, James. Traditional Knitting Patterns. New York: Dover Publications, Inc., 1973.

Royce, Beverly. Notes on Double Knitting. Pittsville: Schoolhouse Press, 1994.

Stanfield, Lesley. The New Knitting Stitch Library. Radnor: Chilton Book Co., 1992.

Thomas, Mary. Mary Thomas's Knitting Book. New York: Dover Publications, Inc., 1938, 1972.

Zimmermann, Elizabeth. Knitter's Almanac. New York: Dover Publications, 1974